Bipolar Disorder

About the Authors

Robert Reiser, PhD, is a Fellow of the Academy of Cognitive Therapy and Director of the Gronowski Psychology Clinic at Pacific Graduate School of Psychology in Palo Alto, CA, where he supervises graduate psychologists in training, teaches classes in cognitive behavioral therapy, and provides workshops, consultation, and technical assistance related to improvements in the treatment of bipolar disorder in community mental health settings. Dr. Reiser's primary clinical and research interests involve developing and implementing evidence-based treatments in a range of community and clinic settings.

Larry W. Thompson, PhD, received his doctorate from Florida State University in 1951. Since then he has held the rank of Professor at three universities, Duke University, University of Southern California, and Stanford University. Dr. Thompson's recent interests have focused on the problems and issues involved in transporting evidenced-based psychotherapeutic interventions from the research laboratory into community settings.

Advances in Psychotherapy – Evidence-Based Practice

Danny Wedding; PhD, MPH, Prof., St. Louis, MO
(Series Editor)
Larry Beutler; PhD, Prof., Palo Alto, CA
Kenneth E. Freedland; PhD, Prof., St. Louis, MO
Linda C. Sobell; PhD, ABPP, Prof., Ft. Lauderdale, FL
David A. Wolfe; PhD, Prof., Toronto
(Associate Editors)

The basic objective of this new series is to provide therapists with practical, evidence-based treatment guidance for the most common disorders seen in clinical practice – and to do so in a "reader-friendly" manner. Each book in the series is both a compact "how-to-do" reference on a particular disorder for use by professional clinicians in their daily work, as well as an ideal educational resource for students and for practice-oriented continuing education.
The most important feature of the books is that they are practical and "reader-friendly": All are structured similarly and all provide a compact and easy-to-follow guide to all aspects that are relevant in real-life practice. Tables, boxed clinical "pearls", marginal notes, and summary boxes assist orientation, while checklists provide tools for use in daily practice.

The series *Advances in Psychotherapy – Evidence-Based Practice* has been developed and is edited with the support of the Society of Clinical Psychology (APA Division 12). The Society is planning a system of home study continuing education courses based on the series that an individual can complete on the web.

Bipolar Disorder

Robert P. Reiser
Pacific Graduate School of Psychology, Palo Alto, CA

Larry W. Thompson
Pacific Graduate School of Psychology, Palo Alto, CA

HOGREFE

BS

Library of Congress Cataloging in Publication

is available via the Library of Congress Marc Database under the
LC Control Number 2005927215

Library and Archives Canada Cataloguing in Publication

Reiser, Robert P.
    Bipolar disorder / Robert P. Reiser, Larry W. Thompson.

(Advances in psychotherapy--evidence-based practice)
Includes bibliographical references.
ISBN 0-88937-310-8

    1. Manic-depressive illness. I. Thompson, Larry W. II. Title. III. Series.

RC516.R45 2005   616.89'5   C2005-903033-X

© 2005 by Hogrefe & Huber Publishers

PUBLISHING OFFICES
USA: Hogrefe & Huber Publishers, 875 Massachusetts Avenue, 7th Floor,
                Cambridge, MA 02139
                Phone (866) 823-4726, Fax (617) 354-6875, E-mail info@hhpub.com
EUROPE: Hogrefe & Huber Publishers, Rohnsweg 25, 37085 Göttingen, Germany
                Phone +49 551 49609-0, Fax +49 551 49609-88, E-mail hh@hhpub.com

SALES & DISTRIBUTION
USA: Hogrefe & Huber Publishers, Customer Services Department,
                30 Amberwood Parkway, Ashland, OH 44805
                Phone (800) 228-3749, Fax (419) 281-6883, E-mail custserv@hhpub.com
EUROPE: Hogrefe & Huber Publishers, Rohnsweg 25, 37085 Göttingen, Germany
                Phone +49 551 49609-0, Fax +49 551 49609-88, E-mail hh@hhpub.com

OTHER OFFICES
CANADA: Hogrefe & Huber Publishers, 1543 Bayview Avenue, Toronto, Ontario M4G 3B5
SWITZERLAND: Hogrefe & Huber Publishers, Länggass-Strasse 76, CH-3000 Bern 9

Hogrefe & Huber Publishers
Incorporated and registered in the State of Washington, USA, and in Göttingen, Lower Saxony,
Germany

Printed and bound in the USA
ISBN 0-88937-310-8

u\7\08

Preface

After several decades of relative neglect, the past 10 years has seen a dramatic increase of interest in the psychosocial treatment of bipolar disorder. With mounting evidence for the effectiveness of several treatment approaches to this disorder, there is a significant opportunity to improve understanding and clinical treatment of bipolar disorder for the everyday practitioner. Unfortunately, this plethora of research has only made limited contributions to everyday clinical practice, resulting in a widening gap between what we know to be effective and the actual standard of care delivered in the community. This observation is consistent with the overall picture presented in the National Institute of Mental Health (NIMH) white paper on research in mood disorders, which finds that only about 10% of treatment for depression (a far more common affective disorder) meets the standard for guideline level care.

At this point there is a daunting amount of information that can be gleaned from research studies, systematic literature reviews, and treatment manuals that is not readily accessible to the practitioner. This guide seeks to present a series of evidence-based approaches to the treatment of bipolar disorder while trying to avoid an overly specialized approach or a set of highly complex procedures. We have also attempted to address important problems likely to be encountered with more challenging patients typically seen in a variety of common treatment settings such as community mental health clinics. This book attempts to bring to the practitioner an evidence-based, comprehensive, integrated approach to the treatment of bipolar disorder that is practical, easily accessible, and can be readily applied in clinical practice.

Assumptions for Use of this Book

This book presents a collateral psychosocial treatment that does not substitute for standard psychiatric care. The treatment program presented here is designed to provide supplemental treatment and support for individuals who are receiving standard psychiatric care and medication management. Ongoing treatment with a recognized mood stabilizer should be a requirement of participation in any psychosocial treatment program. Accepting patients with bipolar disorder who are not under current psychiatric care presents a serious risk and is contraindicated in most cases.

This guide assumes that the reader has some knowledge of treating individuals with more serious mental disorders. As these individuals are often seen in community settings we specifically discuss adapting treatment strategies to minimize attrition, address motivational issues, and maximize gains for complex multi-disordered patients in diverse, multi-disciplinary, community-based settings.

Acknowledgments

Both authors wish to thank The Health Trust, a nonprofit foundation and community resource in San Jose, California, which generously supported their work with bipolar disorder in community mental health settings over a 2-year period. The first author dedicates this book to the memory of his mother, Antoinette Overly; and to his life-long companion and wife, Susan, and his three wonderful sons Evan, Spencer, and Luke. He also wishes to also acknowledge the ongoing supervision, assistance, and mentorship of Monica Basco and the support of Ellen Frank. The second author wishes to acknowledge the value of his wife's ongoing love and support. Both authors would like to also recognize Shilpa Reddy, Tam Nguyen, and Lauren Durkin for assembling the literature review and assisting in final edits. We are both also indebted to our patients and our students who have been our best teachers.

Robert P. Reiser
Larry W. Thompson

Table of Contents

Description

1.1 Terminology

Bipolar disorder [previously known as Manic Depressive Reaction (DSM-I) and Manic Depressive Illness (DSM-II)] is a mood disorder characterized by a long-term episodic cyclical course of extreme fluctuations in mood resulting in significant impairment in social, interpersonal, and occupational functioning.

In the current diagnostic nomenclature, bipolar disorder falls within the broader mood disorders diagnostic grouping, which is divided into major depressive disorders and bipolar disorders. The *Diagnostic and Statistical Manual of Mental Disorders*, Fourth Edition, Text Revision (DSM-IV-TR; American Psychiatric Association, 2000) and the World Health Organization *International Classification of Diseases* (Maier & Sandmann, 1993) have adopted a classification system (see Appendix 1) that emphasizes the categorical nature of unipolar and bipolar disorders. This classification schema provides significant improvements in differential diagnosis and establishes higher levels of interobserver reliability for specific diagnoses at the expense of overemphasizing a dichotomous view of mood disorders. In the DSM-IV-TR classification system, mood disorders are effectively divided into two categorical groups – the depressive disorders and the bipolar disorders – that are distinguished primarily by the presence or absence of a *history* of manic episodes, mixed episodes, or hypomanic episodes.

Bipolar disorders are grouped into four mutually exclusive categories depending upon the presence or absence of manic, mixed and hypomanic episodes: bipolar I disorder, bipolar II disorder, cyclothymic disorder, and bipolar disorder not otherwise specified.

Bipolar I disorder is characterized by one or more manic or mixed episodes of sufficient severity to cause marked impairment in social and occupational functioning most often resulting in a psychiatric hospitalization.

Bipolar II disorder is characterized by one or more major depressive episodes with at least one hypomanic episode in which the patient's functioning is not compromised severely enough to cause marked impairment in social or occupational functioning.

Cyclothymic disorder is characterized by mood instability over a 2-year period with hypomanic and depressed symptoms that do not meet full criteria for a manic episode or a major depressive episode.

Bipolar disorder not otherwise specified is used to identify bipolar disorders that do not meet the criteria cited above due to failure to meet criteria for duration or clustering of symptoms, or due to lack of confirmatory information for establishing a diagnosis.

1.2   Definition

Bipolar disorders are distinguished from other mood disorders primarily by the presence or absence of a *history* of **manic episodes**, **mixed episodes**, or **hypomanic episodes**. These are essentially the basic "building blocks" that allow practitioners to make a differential diagnosis. Table 1 presents the criteria for a diagnosis of a **major depressive episode** as described in the DSM-IV-TR. Table 2 presents the criteria for a **manic episode** as described in the DSM-

Table 1
Criteria for a Major Depressive Episode Taken Directly from DSM-IV-TR

A. Five (or more) of the following symptoms have been present during the same 2-week period and represent a change from previous functioning; at least one of the symptoms is either (1) depressed mood or (2) loss of interest or pleasure. *Note:* Do not include symptoms that are clearly due to a general medical condition, or mood-incongruent delusions or hallucinations.

  1. Depressed mood most of the day, nearly every day, as indicated by either subjective report (e.g., feels sad or empty) or observation made by others (e.g., appears tearful). *Note:* In children and adolescents, can be irritable mood.
  2. Markedly diminished interest or pleasure in all, or almost all, activities most of the day, nearly every day (as indicated by either subjective account or observation made by others)
  3. Significant weight loss when not dieting or weight gain (e.g., a change of more than 5% of body weight in a month), or decrease or increase in appetite nearly every day. *Note:* In children, consider failure to make expected weight gains.
  4. Insomnia or hypersomnia nearly every day
  5. Psychomotor agitation or retardation nearly every day (observable by others, not merely subjective feelings of restlessness or being slowed down)
  6. Fatigue or loss of energy nearly every day
  7. Feelings of worthlessness or excessive or inappropriate guilt (which may be delusional) nearly every day (not merely self-reproach or guilt about being sick)
  8. Diminished ability to think or concentrate, or indecisiveness, nearly every day (either by subjective account or as observed by others)
  9. Recurrent thoughts of death (not just fear of dying), recurrent suicidal ideation without a specific plan, or a suicide attempt or a specific plan for committing suicide

B. The symptoms do not meet criteria for a mixed episode

C. The symptoms cause clinically significant distress or impairment in social, occupational, or other important areas of functioning.

D. The symptoms are not due to the direct physiological effects of a substance (e.g., a drug of abuse, a medication) or a general medical condition (e.g., hypothyroidism).

E. The symptoms are not better accounted for by bereavement, i.e., after the loss of a loved one, the symptoms persist for longer than 2 months or are characterized by marked functional impairment, morbid preoccupation with worthlessness, suicidal ideation, psychotic symptoms, or psychomotor retardation.

IV-TR. Manic-like episodes that are clearly caused by somatic antidepressant treatment (e.g., medication, electroconvulsive therapy, light therapy) should not count toward a diagnosis of bipolar I disorder. Table 3 presents the criteria for a **mixed episode** as described in the DSM-IV-TR. As with manic episodes, mixed episodes that are caused by somatic antidepressant treatment should not

Criteria for manic episode

Table 2
Criteria for Manic Episode Taken Directly from DSM-IV-TR

A. A distinct period during which there is an abnormally and persistently elevated, expansive or irritable mood lasting at least 1 week (or less if hospitalization is necessary).

B. During the period of mood disturbance, *three* or more of the following have persisted (*four* if mood is only irritable) and have been present to a significant degree:

1. Inflated selfesteem or grandiosity
2. Decreased need for sleep (e.g., feels rested after only 3 hours of sleep)
3. More talkative then usual or pressure to keep talking
4. flight of ideas or subjective experience that thoughts are racing
5. Distractibility (attention too easily drawn to unimportant or irrelevant external stimuli)
6. Increased involvement in goal-directed activity (either socially, at work or school, or sexually) or psychomotor agitation
7. Excessive involvement in pleasurable activities that have a high potential for painful consequences (e.g., engaging in unrestrained buying sprees, sexual indiscretions, or foolish business investments)

C. The symptoms do not meet the criteria for a mixed episode.

D. The mood disturbance is sufficiently severe to cause marked impairment in occupational functioning or in usual social activities or relationships with others, or to necessitate hospitalization to prevent harm to self or others, or there are psychotic features.

E. The symptoms are not due to the direct physiological effects of a substance (e.g., drug of abuse, a medication, or other treatment) or a general medical condition (e.g., hyperthyroidism).

Criteria for mixed episode

Table 3
Criteria for the Diagnosis of a Mixed Episode Taken Directly from DSM-IV-TR

A. The criteria are met for both a manic episode and for a major depressive episode (except for duration) nearly every day during at least a 1-week period.

B. The mood disturbance is sufficiently severe to cause marked impairment in occupational functioning or in usual social activities or relationships with others, or to necessitate hospitalization to prevent harm to self or others, or there are psychotic features.

C. The symptoms are not due to the direct physiological effects of a substance (e.g. a drug of abuse, a medication, or other treatment) or a general medical condition (e.g., hyperthyroidism).

count toward a diagnosis of bipolar I disorder. Table 4 presents the criteria for a **hypomanic episode** as described in the DSM-IV-TR. As with manic episodes and mixed episodes, hypomanic episodes that are caused by somatic antidepressant treatment should not count toward a diagnosis of bipolar II disorder.

1.2.1 Additional Considerations in the Classification and Diagnosis of Bipolar Disorders

It should be noted that many authors now believe that the classification system discussed above has unfairly compromised a more unitary view of mood disorders, with the result that the entire clinical spectrum of bipolar disorder is underrecognized, underdiagnosed, and undertreated. This narrower definition of bipolar disorder establishes a number of arbitrary thresholds (e.g., **bipolar I** versus **bipolar II**) based on duration and clustering of symptoms that may not effectively identify individuals who are experiencing subsyndromal symptoms with significant functional impairments, and who may be at higher risk for dysthymic disorder, comorbid anxiety disorders, subsyndromal depression, and suicide.

Criteria for
hypomanic episode

Table 4
Criteria for the Diagnosis of a Hypomanic Episode Taken Directly from DSM-IV-TR

A. A distinct period of persistently elevated, expansive or irritable mood lasting throughout at least 4 days that is clearly different from the usual nondepressed mood.

B. During the period of mood disturbance, *three* (or more) of the following have persisted (*four* if mood is only irritable) and have been present to a significant degree:
   1. Inflated selfesteem or grandiosity
   2. Decreased need for sleep (e.g. feels rested after only 3 hours of sleep)
   3. More talkative then usual or pressure to keep talking
   4. Flight of ideas or subjective experience that thoughts are racing
   5. Distractibility (attention too easily drawn to unimportant or irrelevant external stimuli)
   6. Increased involvement in goal-directed activity (either socially, at work or school, or sexually) or psychomotor agitation
   7. Excessive involvement in pleasurable activities that have a high potential for painful consequences (e.g., engaging in unrestrained buying sprees, sexual indiscretions, or foolish business investments)

C. The episode is associated with an unequivocal change in functioning that is uncharacteristic of the person when not symptomatic.

D. The disturbance in mood and change in functioning are observable by others.

E. The episode is not severe enough to cause marked impairment in social or occupational functioning, or to necessitate hospitalization, and there are no psychotic features.

F. The symptoms are not due to the direct physiological effects of a substance (e.g., a drug of abuse, a medication, or other treatment) or a general medical condition (e.g., hyperthyroidism).

Indeed, a recent study (Post, Leverich, Altshuler, Frye, Suppes, Keck, et al., 2003) provides extremely compelling empirical evidence that patients experience significant subsyndromal mood fluctuations in functioning and significant levels of impairment outside of severe episodes. This report examined morbidity in 258 bipolar outpatients who completed daily ratings of mood and impairment level for a period of 1 year. For patients in this group, 26.4% were characterized as severely ill (with severe impairments during more than 75% of the time during the year) and only 32.9% of this cohort was considered "relatively well." These data and other findings have led authors to argue for a more unitary view of mood disorders that essentially distributes all mood disorders along a bipolar spectrum. This less categorical view of mood disorders deemphasizes the distinctions between unipolar and bipolar depression and between bipolar I and bipolar II disorders.

Many patients experience significant impairment between episodes

1.2.2   Implications for Clinical Practice

The concept of a broader bipolar spectrum of mood disorders has significant implications for clinical practice as follows:

1. *Improved screening for bipolar disorders.* In reviews of the incidence of "less than manic" forms of bipolar disorders, prevalence rates of approximately 5% of the population have been reported versus approximately 1% for mania as defined by DSM-IV-TR thresholds. This should alert the practitioner to improve screening procedures in order to detect this far higher rate of bipolar disorders in the population than might be identified by imposing strict DSM-IV-TR criteria. More sensitive screening can lead to:

    a. *Improved quality of lives for patients and families.* A number of studies have documented significant decrements in quality of life for individuals with bipolar disorder and their families. Earlier recognition and treatment of bipolar spectrum disorders can contribute to reducing family burden and improving patient's lives.

    b. *Reduced risk of suicide.* Both bipolar I and bipolar II disorders are associated with increased risk of lifetime suicide. Bipolar II disorders may actually have a more chronic depressive course with more significant depressive episodes than bipolar I disorders and hence should receive equally aggressive treatment.

    Suicide risk is higher in bipolar II disorder

    c. *Reduced risk of comorbid substance abuse.* The rate of comorbid substance abuse disorders in bipolar disorder is among the highest of any axis I disorder and greatly complicates treatment in part by reducing treatment compliance. Early recognition and treatment, may reduce the risk of comorbid substance abuse disorders.

    Rates of comorbid substance abuse extremely high

2. *Improving the diagnosis of bipolar depression.* Approximately 60% of all patients with bipolar disorder present with an initial depressive phase episode. In one sample of patients followed for 15 years, approximately 27% of patients hospitalized for a major depressive episode went on to develop hypomania and 17% had a manic episode. In another analysis, Benazzi and Akiskal (2003) noted that up to 50% of patients presenting with a major depressive episode may have a bipolar II type disorder if "less than manic"

    Most patients present in the depressed phase

forms of bipolar disorder are considered. By deemphasizing differences between unipolar and bipolar disorders, the clinician will be sensitized to the need for extremely careful assessment of all depressive presentations to rule out bipolar disorder. Misdiagnosis has critical implications for treatment in that treatment with an antidepressant may worsen bipolar depression or induce mania.

3. *Improving treatment for bipolar II disorders.* Bipolar II disorders should not simply be viewed as subthreshold or "light" versions of bipolar I disorders. In fact, bipolar II disorders may have a more pernicious course in terms of duration of depressive phase episodes and cause significant impairment in functioning and reduced quality of life in interpersonal, social, and occupational domains.

1.3   Epidemiology

Prevalence rates for bipolar spectrum disorders between 2.6% and 7.8%

A summary of earlier work suggested that the lifetime prevalence of bipolar disorder in the United States was about 1.2% (Goodwin & Jamison, 1990). A more recent review of studies completed within the past decade reported that lifetime prevalence may range from 2.6% to 7.8% when the full bipolar spectrum is considered (Rihmer & Angst, 2005). These authors also reported that the lifetime prevalence rate for bipolar I and bipolar II alone ranged from 0.3% to 7.2%. The increased rate across this span of time more than likely reflects greater attention to improved assessment practices and more refined diagnostic precision. Recent work has emphasized the importance of briefer (< 4 days) hypomanic episodes that occur intermittently with depression, along with greater concern about other subsyndromal symptoms occurring in between episodes. The clinician is cautioned that formal changes in diagnostic criteria and classification schemes are likely to be forthcoming in the near future as a result of this work. These changes will be more in line with recent conceptualizations of bipolarity as a spectrum disorder, ranging from predominant depression with intermittent hypomania to predominant mania (Akiskal et al., 2000; Judd & Akiskal, 2003). However, for the present, the nosological distinctions outlined in the DSM-IV-TR are considered as still useful in categorizing patients (Judd, Akiskal, Schettler, Coryell, Maser, Rice, et al., 2003).

A major cause of disability and suicide

Although the prevalence rate for bipolar disorder is less than that for other mood disorders, it is a major cause of disability (Thomas, 2004). As might be expected, the economic burden for families, health care programs, and industry is immense. Some authors have argued that bipolar disorder may be the most costly psychiatric disorder in the United States (Peele, Xu, & Kupfer, 2003). The psychological toll on families and friends of bipolar patients is also of major importance. Often the economic and emotional stresses of attempting to deal with the problems caused by these individuals eventually become so great that family members and other loved ones become overwhelmed. It is estimated that one-fourth to more than one-half of bipolar patients make at least one medically serious suicide attempt, and roughly 10% – 20% are successful in their attempt (Post & Altshuler, 2005).

In contrast to unipolar depression, in which the disorder occurs nearly twice as often in women than in men, the prevalence rate of bipolar depression is approximately the same in males and females when all subtypes are considered. However, if one looks at subtypes within the bipolar spectrum, then there are a greater proportion of females as the depression component becomes more predominant, whereas in the mania end of the continuum there are notably more males than females.

The onset of bipolar disorder tends to occur around age 20, with approximately 50% of patients having their first episode before this age. This is about 10 years younger than the onset of unipolar depression. Initial onset in older individuals above 60 years of age is seldom seen. This was also thought to be the case with prepubertal and early adolescent bipolar disorder. More recently, evidence has been accumulating that this diagnostic phenotype is appropriate, and while it shares some symptoms with attention deficit hyperactivity disorder (ADHD), there are sufficient differences to argue that it should be considered a distinct diagnostic classification from ADHD (Tillman, Geller, Bolhofner, Craney, Williams, & Zimerman, 2003). Others, however, have reported that preadolescent mania is not on a continuum with adult mania, and argue that more work is needed before any conclusions can be drawn (Harrington & Myatt, 2003). Patients with a positive family history of mood disorders usually have their first episode at an earlier age and episodes are precipitated by fewer stressors than in those patients who have no family history of a mood disorder (Rihmer & Angst, 2005).

Mean age of onset typically is 20

50% of patients by definition are diagnosed before 20th birthday

It is commonly accepted that cultural factors may affect the syndromal pattern of both depression and mania. However, epidemiologic studies in the United States suggest that the differences in bipolar disorder observed between Caucasians, Hispanic Americans, and African Americans may be accounted for by differences in socioeconomic factors. There clearly is a relationship between harsh environmental conditions and the frequency and intensity of episodes, but it may be the case that more severe episodes, particularly manic episodes, lead to unemployment, low income, divorce, loss of emotional and instrumental support systems, and less opportunity for educational and professional training. The potential for a devastating reciprocal interaction between the disorder and stressful environmental conditions suggested here is frequently in evidence among patients diagnosed with bipolar I disorder. In bipolar II patients the hypomanic episodes may be less disruptive, and this may contribute to their higher socioeconomic status (Rihmer & Angst, 2005).

Family history appears to be one of the most influential risk factors for the development of a mood disorder, particularly for bipolar disorder (Merikangas & Low, 2004). For example, the average risk ratio, calculated from values obtained in four well-controlled studies, for bipolar disorder among relatives of bipolar probands (10.3) is similar to the risk ratio for many diseases known to have a genetic basis. The magnitude of this ratio is nearly 3 times greater than the average risk ratio for major depressive disorder (3.6), which suggests only a moderate genetic influence. Twin studies provide even more compelling evidence that mood disorders have hereditary influences, and furthermore bipolar disorder shows a much higher involvement of genetic influence in the etiology (.59) than does unipolar disorder (.37). These values indicate that

Stronger genetic basis for bipolar disorder than major depression

substantially less influence can be attributed to heritability (roughly one-third) in the etiology of unipolar disorder. Attempts to look at possible familial or genetic differences in subtypes along the bipolar spectrum or gender differences have shown some inconsistencies and few conclusions can be drawn at the present time.

1.4   Course and Prognosis

Highly variable course with predominance of depressive episodes

The course of bipolar disorder can be quite variable, depending on the subtype. The subtypes are described in greater detail in a later section. Briefly, the symptom pattern can range from predominant depression with occasional brief periods of hypomania to chronic hypermania with the occasional appearance of severe manic episodes. Episodes can be of varying duration and frequency, ranging from a single lifetime manic episode that persists over an extended period of weeks or months to multiple cycling from mania to depression within a single 24-hour period. The severity of both depressive and manic episodes can also range from a mild state, causing only minor perturbations in functioning, to a severe form, resulting in marked functional impairment with psychotic features. As more has been learned about bipolar disorder, clinicians and researchers are beginning to view this disorder on a single continuum ranging from mild to more severe bipolar states with interspersed depressive episodes of variable length, rather than the discrete subtype categories as described in later sections (Akiskal, 2005).

However, at the present time most of the research has focused on correlates or characteristic features of the subtypes as outlined in DSM-IV-TR. In particular, interest has focused primarily on the bipolar I and bipolar II subtypes, which share a number of similarities as well as differences. For example, in a prospective longitudinal multisite study of depressive disorders over a 10-year period (Judd et al., 2003) it was observed that bipolar I and bipolar II patients had similar demographic characteristics. Both subgroups had substantially higher lifetime prevalence of substance abuse disorder than the general population, though this is somewhat higher in bipolar I patients. The initial lifetime episode was depression in roughly 60% of the patients in both groups and depression was the predominant feature of the illness in both subtypes throughout the follow-up period. As noted earlier, such similarities led the authors to argue that the two are related and lie in different positions along a bipolar spectrum.

On the other hand, a number of differences between the two subtypes were observed in this study. As expected, manic episodes in bipolar I patients are more severe than in bipolar II, and more often result in hospitalization with aggressive somatic treatment. Bipolar I patients can often present with psychotic features, whereas these are less likely in bipolar II patients. However, in the prospective study noted above, roughly 18% of the bipolar II patents were experiencing some psychotic symptoms during the intake episode. Contrary to what one might think, duration of episodes is longer in bipolar II patients, they occur more frequently than in bipolar I patients, and there is less chance that bipolar II patients will recover to their premorbid level following an episode.

Bipolar II patients frequently have comorbid anxiety disorders, whereas bipolar I patients have a prevalence rate of anxiety that is near the rate for the general population. Intermittent wellness periods (i.e., periods when patients are virtually free of manic or depressive symptoms) between episodes are shorter in bipolar II than in bipolar I periods.

In summary, bipolar II disorder can be viewed as more chronic with a greater prevalence of depressive episodes when compared with bipolar I. Some researchers have questioned whether this might be an artifact due to treatment differences, since bipolar I patients are more likely to receive treatment in between episodes than are bipolar II patients (Judd et al., 2003).

Bipolar II has greater prevalence of depressed episodes and higher risk of suicide

Patients diagnosed with bipolar disorder typically have recurring episodes over their lifetime. Even with pharmacologic treatment as outlined by American Psychiatric Association (APA) guidelines, patients continue to experience relentless occurrences of emotional upheavals that often interfere with day to day functioning. Without treatment this disorder can be devastating, resulting in major disruptions in functioning accompanied by substantial losses of friends, family and finances. The high degree of comorbidity associated with this disorder can make the prognosis even worse. The magnitude of the problems here is well illustrated in the findings of the Stanley Foundation Bipolar Network (Post et al., 2003). This multisite treatment program implemented aggressive, highly flexible pharmacotherapy strategies to address the mood disorders and other comorbid conditions. Using the NIMH-Life Chart Methodology (Denticoff, Leverich, Nolen, Rush, McElroy, Keck, & Suppes, 2000), these researchers followed more than 600 patients in treatment over a 30-month time span. The results indicated that two-thirds of the bipolar outpatients continued to be affected by their illness. In one set of 549 patients who had been on antidepressants only about 15% were qualified as being well for a 2-month period. Others in the study failed to respond or switched into a mania episode. While it is clear that some patients responded well in this "state-of-the-art" study, the results leave much room for improvement. Findings such as these emphasize that while pharmacotherapy, as presently practiced, is essential, it is not sufficient to eliminate symptoms completely or result in significantly improved functioning for extended time periods. The addition of psychotherapy designed to help patients deal with problems of living can improve the course of this illness.

Comorbidity results in poorer outcomes

Pharmacotherapy alone is often insufficient

1.5　Differential Diagnosis

The aim of this section is to give practitioners and therapists practical advice on differentiating **bipolar I** and **bipolar II disorders** from **major depressive disorders, psychotic disorders, substance induced mood disorders, mood disorders due to general medical condition, borderline personality disorder, attention deficit disorders** and **conduct disorders**.

For quick reference, the name of each alternative diagnosis is given in bold, followed by:
a) Signs / symptoms / syndromes / characteristics that both have in common
b) Characteristics that differ between the disorders

This section will highlight criteria, key signs and symptoms, family and patient history, and other qualitative factors for differentiating bipolar disorders from other, similar symptom patterns. This is a relatively complex task, due to the substantial degree of comorbid disorders found in patients with bipolar disorder. In a recent review article, it was suggested that approximately two-thirds of patients with bipolar disorder have a second lifetime Axis I disorder.

1.5.1 Differential Diagnosis of Bipolar I and II Disorders Versus Major Depressive Disorders

While it may appear that major depressive disorder (MDD) is readily identified and easily differentiated from bipolar disorder I and II (BDI and I), this area of differential diagnosis probably accounts for the most serious and significant problems that patients with BD I or II experience in terms of misdiagnosis and improper treatment. The differential implications for treatment are highly significant, in that providing an antidepressant to a patient with BD I or II while the patient is in an episode of depression, without a mood stabilizer, greatly increases the risk of inducing an episode of mania or hypomania. Table 5 lists several common and differential features to aid in the distinction between MDD and BD I and II.

A great majority of patients with BD I or II initially present in a depressed phase and a majority of patients with BD I or II experience significant periods of depression between manic, mixed or hypomanic episodes. As noted above, for a variety of reasons patients who are currently in a depressed phase are likely to underreport past histories of both mania and hypomania. Careful history taking supplemented by family members and significant others is a key to proper diagnosis. Because of the chronic and cyclical nature of mood disorders, a longitudinal rather than a crosssectional approach for assessment can be immensely helpful. An excellent supplement to enhance information gathering is the Life Chart Methodology – LCM (Denticoff et al., 2000) – a

Differential diagnosis: Bipolar I versus major depression

Table 5
Differential Diagnosis of Bipolar Disorder (BD I and II) Versus Major Depressive Disorder (MDD)

A. Characteristics that differ between the disorders
   – Earlier age of onset (BD > MDD)
   – More acute onset (BD > MDD)
   – More frequent episodes (BD > MDD)
   – Greater likelihood of psychotic features (BD > MDD)
   – Greater likelihood of atypical features including psychomotor retardation, agitation, and hypersomnia (BD > MDD)
   – Greater likelihood of history of attempted suicide (BD > MDD)
   – Higher rates of family members with manic episodes (BD > MDD)
   – Higher rates of other psychiatric disorders in the family (BD > MDD)
   – Higher rates of comorbid substance disorders (BD > MDD)

standardized data collection instrument that can be used in the interview to help the patient or family members/significant others characterize lifetime patterns of episodes, including hospitalizations, major life events, and use of medication. Interviews spaced over time versus single interviews with patients and significant others increase the sensitivity of the assessment process with little impact on specificity. In the course of therapy, patients can also complete a daily mood chart (See Appendix 4) that tracks mood and other related symptoms (irritability, anxiety, sleep, activity level, etc.). The Life Chart and mood charting in general can be an invaluable aid when there is a diagnostic question as to distinguishing between types of cyclical mood disorders. If the patient is not presenting in a life-threatening crisis, a simplified version of the Life Chart can be mailed out and completed by the patient or family members/significant others prior to the first interview (for further discussion of implementing mood charts with patients and family members see Chapter 4: Treatment).

1.5.2   Differential Diagnosis of Bipolar I Versus Bipolar II Disorder

The differential diagnosis between BD I and BD II is relatively easy to make when the patient presents during a current **manic** or **hypomanic** episode, because of the marked impairment and likelihood of psychotic features associated with **mania.** However, patients often present in a depressed state and information about **mania/hypomania** must be developed by history, using the patient's self-report and other informants (including family and significant others, hospital records where available, and previous treatment records). Table 6 provides characteristics that are common to BD I and II disorders and several that are distinctly different in these two disorders.

Differential diagnosis: Bipolar I versus bipolar II

Table 6
Differential Diagnosis of Bipolar I (BD I) Versus Bipolar II Disorder (BD II)

A. Common signs and symptoms
   − See DSM-IV-TR tables above.

B. Characteristics that distinguish bipolar I and bipolar II disorders
   − Duration of current and past episodes (4 days for BD II versus 7 days for BD I)
   − Severity of current and past episodes especially as indicated by hospitalization or psychotic features (BD I > BD II)
   − Marked impairment during episode (BD I > BD II)
   − More likely to return to baseline functioning between episodes (BD II > BD I)
   − Cyclothymic temperament (BD II > BD I)
   − Greater chronicity of major and minor depressive episodes (BD II > BD I)
   − Higher level of comorbid anxiety disorders (BD II > BD I)
   − Longer duration of less severe episodes (BD II > BD I)
   − Higher risk for suicide (BD II > BD I) (Serretti, 2002)
   − Higher rates of psychomotor retardation, hypersomnia and weight gain during depressive episodes (BD II > BD I) (cited in Serretti, 2002).

1.5.3   Differential Diagnosis of Bipolar I Disorder Versus Psychotic Disorders (Schizoaffective Disorder, Schizophrenia, and Delusional Disorder)

As seen in Table 7, both BD I and psychotic disorder (PD) patients can have grandiose and/or persecutory delusions, as well as extremely disorganized thinking and loose associations, suggestive of a thought disorder. Both are frequently agitated, highly irritable, and may show catatonic symptoms. However, there are a number of distinguishing features between the two diagnostic categories. For example, BD I patients are more likely to have mood-related symptoms than are PD patients. Between episodes BD I patients are less inclined to have psychotic symptoms in the absence of a prominent mood disturbance than are PD patients. BD I patients generally have a higher premorbid level of functioning than do PD patients, lapse into an episode more precipitously than PD patients, and are more likely to return to a premorbid level between episodes. BD I patients are also more likely to have relatives who suffer from BD I or II. When considering these differential features, it is clearly evident that a careful history and evaluation of symptom changes across time should ease the burden of distinguishing between these two categories.

Differential diagnosis: Bipolar I versus psychotic disorders

Table 7
Differential Diagnosis of Bipolar I Disorder (BD I) Versus Psychotic Disorders (PD) (Schizoaffective Disorder, Schizophrenia, and Delusional Disorder)

A. Common signs and symptoms
    – Grandiose or persecutory delusions and hallucinations
    – Disorganized thinking – thought disorder (the accelerated thinking characteristic of mania can lead to loosening of associations and appear to be disorganized)
    – Irritability
    – Agitation
    – Catatonic symptoms

B. Characteristics that distinguish bipolar I and psychotic disorders
    – During the episode, prominent affective, mood-related symptoms (BD > PD)
    – Between episodes, continued presence of psychotic symptoms in the absence of prominent mood symptoms (PD > BD)
    – Family history, first degree relative with bipolar disorder (BD > PD)
    – Higher premorbid functioning (BD > PD)
    – More likely to return to premorbid baseline functioning between episodes (BD > PD)
    – Grossly disorganized behaviors (PD > BD)
    – Insidious onset more likely (PD > BD)

1.5.4   Differential Diagnosis of Bipolar Disorder (Current Episode Manic or Mixed) Versus Substance-Induced Mood Disorder

Both diagnostic categories share a number of mania-like symptoms, but as noted in Table 8, the mood disorder occurs exclusively in association with

Table 8
Differential Diagnosis of Bipolar Disorder (Current Episode Manic or Mixed)
Versus Substance-Induced Mood Disorder

A. Common signs and symptoms
    These disorders may share many symptoms listed under DSM-IV-TR Criterion B
    for **mania** (see Table 3), including elevated, irritable or expansive mood; or, for
    mixed episodes, a combination of symptoms characteristic of **major depressive
    episodes** and **manic episodes** may be present including depressed mood, and
    markedly diminished interest or pleasure in all or most activities.

B. Characteristics that distinguish bipolar I and substance-induced mood
    disorders
    Onset during substance intoxication: Mood disorder occurs exclusively in asso-
    ciation with *intoxication* from alcohol, amphetamines, cocaine, hallucinogens,
    inhalants, phencyclidine, sedatives, hypnotics, other anxiolytics; or unknown
    substances.
    Onset during substance withdrawal: Mood disorder occurs *within 1 month
    of withdrawal* from alcohol, amphetamines, cocaine, hallucinogens, inhal-
    ants, phencyclidine, sedatives, hypnotics, other anxiolytics; or unknown
    substances.

intoxication from alcohol or other substances, such as amphetamines, hal-
lucinogens, inhalants, anxiolytics, etc., or the mood disorder occurs within 1
month following withdrawal from the use of alcohol or other substances.

1.5.5　Differential Diagnosis of Bipolar I and II Disorders Versus Borderline Personality Disorder

Both **borderline personality disorder** (BPD) and BD I or II are characterized
by primary problems with affective instability (difficulty regulating emotions,
also known as emotional dysregulation), impulsivity, and significant periods
of depressive symptoms. In particular, patients with bipolar disorder with
rapid cycling (more than four mood episodes in a 12-month period) may be
inappropriately overdiagnosed as having BPD. Because the diagnostic criteria
for BPD overlap with criteria for mood disorders in terms of symptoms such
as impulsivity, intense anger (primarily during manic phase), reactivity, and
suicidal ideation (primarily during depressed phase), clinicians should avoid
making a differential diagnosis during an acute episode. As with all personality
disorders, **BPD** represents an enduring pattern of behavior, typically with early
onset in adolescence or young adulthood and a long-standing course.

1.5.6　Differential Diagnosis of Bipolar I and II Disorders Versus Attention Deficit Disorders

In a recent review article, Kent and Craddock (2003) compared overlapping
items for **attention deficit with hyperactivity (ADHD)** and BD criteria in
DSM-IV-TR and ICD-10. In summary, there is significant overlap in items
involving hyperactivity, distractibility, and impulsivity. Nonoverlapping items

which can be utilized to discriminate between the disorders are typically associated with *inattention* and mood-related symptoms. For example, patients with **BD I or II** often have inflated self-esteem and ideas of grandiosity. They usually have a decreased need for sleep, and frequently report a rapid flight of ideas that trivializes the requirement for attention to daily routines. Patients with **ADHD,** on the other hand are frequently inattentive without expansiveness and have difficulty sustaining attention even to tasks with high priority.

1.5.7   Differential Diagnosis of Bipolar I and II Disorders Versus Antisocial Personality Disorder

During a **manic episode**, individuals may become excessively involved in pleasure-seeking behaviors (gambling, sexual indiscretions, etc.) and may behave in ways that are reckless, foolish, and cause distress to family members and significant others. Antisocial behavior that occurs exclusively during the course of a **manic episode** should not be diagnosed as **antisocial personality disorder.** The lack of remorse or indifference that characterizes **antisocial personality disorder** can be contrasted with the extreme regret, guilt, and remorse that individuals with BD I or II typically experience at the conclusion of a manic episode.

1.6   Comorbidities

High rates of comorbidity with anxiety disorders, substance abuse and personality disorders

Comorbidity is more the rule than the exception in bipolar disorder. A recent summary of studies focusing on this issue (McIntyre, Konarski, & Yatham, 2004) reported that, "Bipolar disorder may be twice as likely to be accompanied by another lifetime axis I psychiatric disorder than to exist as a singular disorder" (p. 370). Anxiety disorders are 35 times more likely to occur in bipolar patients than in the general population, with 65% – 90% of bipolar patients reporting this disorder during their lifetime. Among all psychiatric disorders, patients with bipolar disorder have the highest prevalence for a substance abuse disorder. In one large survey study, over 60% of bipolar patients reported alcohol dependence and 40% reported drug dependence (Kessler, 1999). McIntyre and his associates (McIntyre, Konarski, & Yatham, 2004) reported that the lifetime prevalence of personality disorders for bipolar patients ranges from 29% to 48%. The following personality disorders were found to have the highest prevalence: obsessive-compulsive, borderline, narcissistic, and avoidant. Other medical problems that are often contributory to mortality, including endocrine, cardiovascular, respiratory, gastrointestinal, and urogenital, occur from more than one to five times more frequently in bipolar patients than in the general population. Diabetes occurs in roughly 10% of bipolar patients, compared to approximately 3% in the general population. Mortality due to cardiovascular disease is twice as likely to occur in bipolar patients as in the general population. Obesity and overweight may be contributory risk factors. In several surveys summarized by McIntyre and associates, 31% – 35% of bipolar patients were overweight and 25% – 34%

Medical comorbidity: Diabetes, obesity, overweight

of these patients were obese. The implications of comorbidity for treatment are clear. Comorbidity complicates the course of the disorder and must be one of the targets in treatment. The multidimensional nature of this disorder thus emphasizes the need for close collaboration with individuals in medicine, psychiatry, and other health-related professions when implementing a treatment program.

1.7   Diagnostic Procedures and Documentation

This section reviews objective tests, diagnostic criteria, and diagnostic procedures relevant to bipolar disorder: (a) for determining the severity of the disorder; and (b) for documenting the course of the disorder or treatment success.

There is no definitive test or laboratory finding to confirm the diagnosis of bipolar disorder. However, as noted previously, it is especially important that clinicians screen carefully for the presence of manic and hypomanic episodes in patients presenting with depression. Most highly complex research-based assessment protocols, including the DSM-IV Structured Clinical Interview (SCID) for axis I disorders, are beyond the scope of ordinary clinic or outpatient practices. However, there are a number of useful screening instruments and checklists for both depression and bipolar disorder.

1.7.1   Tools to Assist in the Assessment of Bipolar Disorder: Mania

The NIMH Life Chart Method (NIMH-LCM)

The Life Chart Method is a graphic tool that helps patients and therapists develop a retrospective (and prospective) look at the course of illness, including major episodes, hospitalizations, significant life events, and medication responsiveness. Because longitudinal assessment is more effective diagnostically than a cross-sectional approach, the Life Chart is an ideal vehicle for capturing historical data in a simplified graphic form that is readily accessible to both patient and therapist. It often provides an important insight into the role of medication, medication response, and treatment compliance in past episodes. Typically, the Life Chart will include all episodes of mania and depression rated on a three point scale – mild (no functional impairment), moderate (distinct functional impairment), and severe (functionally incapacitated – hospitalized). A simplified version of this tool can be provided to patients as a part of the assessment process and the clinician can help the patient review relevant history. A number of clinicians include this routinely in their practice as both an assessment and treatment tool with the rationale that it enhances treatment compliance, collaboration and active participation by the patient (Life Charts are available at http://www.bipolarnews.org).

Diagnostic tools: NIMH Life Chart

The Systematic Treatment Enhancement Program for Bipolar Disorder (STEP-BD), a 5-year NIMH-funded multi-site research program on bipolar

Diagnostic tools from STEP program

disorder, has developed standardized record-keeping forms in an effort to improve clinical assessment and to increase the reliability of the diagnosis of bipolar disorder. These documents make an excellent point of reference for the clinic or individual clinician in developing a more standardized assessment for bipolar disorder.

The STEP-BD Affective Disorders Evaluation (ADE)

The Affective Disorders Evaluation (ADE) is a standardized initial clinical assessment format developed as a part of STEP-BD. While full utilization of the ADE is probably unrealistic for many clinic and outpatient providers, this assessment instrument provides a useful outline that may be adopted for initial clinical assessment in most settings.

The STEP-BD Waiting Room Self-Monitoring and Clinical Monitoring Form (CMF)

The STEP-BD program has also developed a set of standardized record-keeping forms to document clinical progress in a self-report and clinician progress note format. Both of these forms, as well as the ADE, are available for reference along with instructions at http://www.manicdepressive.org, courtesy of Dr. Gary Sachs, the Principle Investigator for STEP-BD.

In addition, Sachs (2004) presents a "Bipolarity Index" that attempts to assign a confidence rating to a diagnosis of bipolar disorder by scoring specific aspects of episode characteristics, age of onset, course of illness, response to treatment and family history in terms of the degree to which these conform to a profile most characteristic of bipolar I disorder. This profile is a useful reference for determining key elements that should be present in your initial clinical assessment. Table 9 summarizes the key characteristics most relevant to bipolar I disorder and is adapted from Sachs (2004, Table 3).

"Bipolarity Index" developed by Sachs

Table 9
"Most Convincing" Characteristics of Bipolar Disorder I (Sachs, 2004)

- Episode Characteristics: Acute manic or mixed episodes with prominent euphoria, grandiosity, or expansiveness (and no known medical etiology)
- First Affective Episode: Age 15–19
- Course of Illness: Recurrent distinct manic episodes with full recovery
- Response to Treatment: Full recovery within 4 weeks on a mood stabilizer
- Family History: At least one first-degree relative with bipolar illness

The Mood Disorder Questionnaire (MDQ)

The Mood Disorder Questionnaire – a key screening tool

For initial screening and recognition of bipolar disorder, the Mood Disorder Questionnaire (Hirschfeld, Williams, Spitzer, Calabrese, Flynn, Keck, et al., 2000) is a simple one-page self-report instrument that can be given to the patient in the waiting room in outpatient clinic settings or private practice settings. The MDQ was compared against the DSM-IV Structured Clinical Interview (SCID), the gold standard for assessment of bipolar disorder in research studies, and provided adequate sensitivity of .73 (indicating that 7 out of 10 people would be correctly identified) and very good specificity of .90 (accurately screening out 9 out of 10 people). The MDQ can be accessed on public websites including the website of the Depression and Bipolar Support Alliance (http://www.dbsalliance.com).

The Young Mania Rating Scale

For assessing the severity of mania specifically and tracking outcomes of treatment, the Young Mania Rating Scale (YMRS) (Young, Biggs, & Ziegler, 1978), a clinician-rated assessment instrument, has good reliability and validity and is a sensitive measure of change in symptoms of mania. The YMRS may not be a first choice for outpatient clinics and private practices, as it requires significant training in order to develop sufficient interrater reliability and takes up to 30 minutes to administer. Unfortunately, there are a limited number of valid and reliable instruments for assessing mania in outpatient populations. The less burdensome self-report measures of mania have not demonstrated sufficient reliability in outpatient populations.

Assessment measures for mania/ hypomania

The Clinical Global Impressions Scale – Bipolar Version (CGI-BP)

The CGI-Bipolar Version (Spearing, Post, & Leverich, 1997) is a version of the Clinical Global Impressions Scale that was developed specifically for Bipolar Disorder and is widely used in clinical trials to assess overall global severity of symptoms in order to assess treatment outcomes for bipolar disorder.

The Altman Self-Rating Scale for Mania (ASRM)

The Altman Self-Rating Scale for Mania (ASRM) (Attman, Hedeker, Peterson, & Davies, 1997) is a very simple 5-item self-report scale that is easy to administer and has demonstrated adequate reliability and validity with inpatient populations and is a sensitive indicator of clinical changes. Using a cutoff score of 6 or higher this rating scale had a sensitivity of 85.5% (indicating it appropriately detected patients with mania 85.5% of the time) and a specificity of 87.5% (accurately identifying patients without mania in 87 out of 100 cases). It provides a simple and useful overall screening for acute mania and a snapshot of current severity. Unfortunately, its use with outpatients has not been sufficiently studied for it to be considered as a primary rating tool.

1.7.2   Tools to Assist in the Assessment of Bipolar Disorder: Depression

Because depression is a key treatment target in patients with bipolar disorder, a number of simple instruments that assess the severity of depression will be reviewed. There are a number of self-report and clinician-administered assessments that have demonstrated good reliability in terms of screening for depression, measuring the severity of depression, and assisting clinicians in tracking outcomes related to depressive symptoms.

Assessment measures for depression

The Hamilton Rating Scale for Depression (HAM-D)

The HAM-D (Williams, 1988) is a clinician-rated scale that is recognized as a "gold standard" for measuring the severity of depression. The HAM-D scale contains items that assess key symptoms of depression, including overall mood, somatic symptoms, insomnia, loss of interest and pleasure, guilt, psychomotor retardation, agitation, and anxiety. The HAM-D offers high validity and reliability and is sensitive to clinical changes in terms of response to treatment. A major drawback of the HAM-D Scale for clinical practice is that it requires training and administration time may exceed 30 minutes for more severely depressed patients.

The Beck Depression Inventory (BDI-II)

For assessing the severity of depression in bipolar disorders, the BDI-II (Beck & Garbin, 1988) revised from an earlier version is a widely used and simple paper-and-pencil self-report checklist that can be completed in the waiting room in 5–7 minutes typically. The BDI-II is a reliable indicator of the overall level of depression, and is clinically sensitive to change. The BDI-II also contains specific items that target the severity of hopelessness and suicide ideation/plans. Items 2 (pessimism) and 9 (suicidal ideation/plans) serve as very useful indicators of overall suicide risk. A "3" or "4" rating on either item should prompt immediate further investigation of current suicide ideation and plans and documentation of a management plan.

The Inventory of Depressive Symptomatology Self Report Version (IDS-SR)

The IDS-SR (Rush, Gullion, & Basco, 1996) is a 28-item self-report multiple-choice questionnaire designed to measure depressive symptomatology in both outpatient and inpatient populations that takes approximately 15 minutes to complete. The IDS-SR has a high level of reliability, internal consistency, and demonstrated validity in terms of correlations with other standardized measures of depression including the Beck Depression Inventory and he Hamilton Rating Scale for Depression. Rush, Giles, and Schlesser (1985) identify the following scoring guidelines for the IDS-SR: scores equal to or above 39 indicate severely depressed; scores between 30 and 38 indicate moderately to severely depressed; scores between 22 and 29 indicate mildly depressed, scores equal to or less than 13 indicate normal mood range.

1.7.3   Taking a good history

The importance of a longitudinal assessment

Because personal and family history is a determining factor in appropriately identifying bipolar disorders and distinguishing them from depressive disorders, single interviews with patients alone are often not reliable in establishing a diagnosis, and ideally the clinician will develop a longitudinal perspective over several interviews, including family members and significant others as historians. The patient's ability to give an adequate history of previous episodes may be compromised by their current mood state as recall of past episodes is influenced by current mood.

While DSM-IV-TR emphasizes current signs and symptoms in determining the diagnosis, history and longitudinal course are the best overall data sources to review in order to make a reliable determination. Goodwin and Jamison (1990) state: "When making a diagnosis, the clinician ideally assesses presenting signs and symptoms and weighs them together with the patient's history and prior response to treatment and the family's history" (page 89).

Clinical Vignette
Identifying Periods of Sleep Loss and Hyperactivity Characteristic of Hypomanic/Manic Episodes

Therapist: Have you ever had any periods where you have needed considerably less sleep than usual for several days in a row?

Patient: Needed or wanted?

Therapist: No, it's more like you haven't felt tired and you didn't feel you needed the sleep.

Patient: Not recently, but within the last several months – yes.

Therapist: For more than a week at a stretch?

Patient: It was about a week. I just wasn't sleeping very much. [Suggests a hypomanic or possibly manic episode]

Therapist: OK. There's a difference between not being able to get to sleep or stay asleep, versus you felt you didn't need the sleep.

Patient: Oh, I was having a lot of trouble sleeping at that time.

Therapist: OK. Were you in a particularly energetic active frame of mind during that time?

Patient: No.

Therapist: Do you feel like you have had any periods of high activity where your mood has been higher or more irritable than normal for an extended period of time?

Patient: No.

This appears to rule out key symptoms of hypomanic episodes – where the patient experienced elevated or irritable mood and sleep loss. In our experience it is rare for patients to have a significant hypomanic episode without sleep loss in the range of getting less than 4–5 hours. Progressive sleep loss is one of the best overall indicators for prodromal risk of hypomania.

Table 10
Assessment of BD I and II: Elements of Taking a Good History

- Utilize multiple interviews and include family members/significant others whenever possible (Goodwin & Jamison, 1990).
- Review family history of first degree relatives – Ask specifically about episodes of mania or hypomania.
- Review any episodes resulting in hospitalization or severe impairment in social or occupational functioning – Inquire about extreme or severe episodes of elevated mood.
- *Always* assess for suicidality, as lifetime suicide risk is extremely high in this population.
- For depressed presentations, carefully assess history, as bipolar disorders cannot be adequately assessed using a cross-sectional methodology alone.
- Have the patient or family members complete a Life Chart that helps establish any acute episodes, date of hospitalizations, major life events, and medication trials (Post, Roy-Byrne, & Uhde, 1988).
- Request medical records for any hospitalization or extended outpatient treatment.

2

Theories and Models of Bipolar Disorder

This section reviews the results of the latest research with a focus on helping the practitioner understand bipolar disorder and explain it effectively to patients within a therapeutic framework likely to motivate the patient. Models and theories presented are linked to practical case examples and case conceptualizations.

The following theoretical models of the disorder are reviewed so that the practitioner can examine and analyze her or his patient's case from each of these different theoretical viewpoints:
1. Biologically based disease models
2. General psychoeducation and illness management strategies
3. The Interpersonal and Social Rhythm Hypothesis: social rhythm disruption as a potential catalyst for bipolar episodes
4. Family-based treatment approaches
5. Cognitive-behavioral treatment approaches

It should be pointed out that there is considerable overlap between the various theories and models of bipolar disorder and that many models share common therapeutic interventions despite differences in theory and approach to the illness. At this stage, there is limited evidence that allows the practitioner to select from these various models on a purely empirical basis.

2.1   Biologically Based Disease Models

Biologically based models of bipolar disorder

An abundance of basic and clinical research has been accumulated over the past three decades that provides compelling evidence for the implication of biological mechanisms in the development of bipolar disorder. For example, a strong case has been made for the presence of a genetic component that may interact with environmental stressors to precipitate the onset of the cyclical mood swings characteristic of bipolar disorder. Leading medical researchers have come to view this disease as symptomatic of "serious brain disorders that have clearly defined motor, mood, cognitive, somatic, neurophysiological, and neurochemical concomitants" (Post & Altshuler, 2005, p. 1662). Precise models that detail specific mechanisms, however, are not yet forthcoming.

A brief review of studies involving various pharmacological treatments leads to some understanding of why this is the case. The effects of different medications are often highly variable and may depend on individual differences that are not yet recognized. Variable effects, which are seen in different studies, await detailed parametric investigations for clarification. Some pharmacological agents that influence different neurochemical systems seem to have similar effects, while others that may impact on one neuroendocrine system selectively in different ways (e.g., a reuptake blocker versus an enzyme inhibitor) may have totally different effects. All this points to the fact that there is no single class of medication that seems to be effective in all cases. Even lithium – the gold standard for mood stabilizers in terms of evidence of long term mood stability – has proven to be completely efficacious in less than 50% of patients who received treatment.

It is now readily accepted that treatment of this complex disorder is exceedingly difficult, and consensus groups to establish guidelines for treatment tend to discount monotherapy strategies (cf. International Consensus Group on Bipolar I Depression Treatment Guidelines, 2004; Post & Altschuler, 2005). The complexities of treatment with such different classes of medications (e.g., antidepressants, anticonvulsants, antipsychotics, mood stabilizers) has made it difficult to develop a model that is highly specific in detailing what are the critical physiological and anatomical factors underlying this disorder. Perhaps the most consistent picture of any observed in the summary of this research is a remnant of the amine hypothesis which stems from the observation that medications leading to excess neurotransmitters in this class are associated with mania, while a lack of these neurotransmitters is believed to lead to depression. However, establishing a treatment regimen based on this model alone has not proven to be completely effective in preventing relapse or recurrence of the disorder.

Given the wide-ranging pharmacological treatment pathways based on drug treatment studies, one might argue that the cluster of symptoms categorized as bipolar disorder may well be the final common pathway of a number of different etiological agents, which in many instances have not yet been identified. This in no way should discount the importance of a biological approach to the treatment of this disease. On the contrary, it highlights the challenges confronting the clinician as he or she attempts to discover that combination of medications which will be maximally effective with each individual patient in the treatment of current and prevention of future episodes.

2.2   General Psychoeducation and Illness Management Strategies

Psychoeducational treatment models of bipolar disorder emphasize a combined diathesis (innate vulnerability) plus stress (environmental factors) approach to psychiatric disorders. This model hypothesizes that both vulnerability to stress and innate biological, genetic factors play a role in the production of episodes of illness. For all serious and chronic mental disorders that are cyclical and episodic in nature (psychotic disorders and mood disorders), it is important to identify protective and risk factors that may be implicated in exacerbations of the illness or new episodes. In fact, most psychosocial treatment approaches to these disorders have proposed underlying models consistent with the diathesis stress model. A purely biological approach does not allow for the full range of

Psychoeducational approaches

The diathesis-stress model for bipolar disorder

patient self-management strategies that would be a given for medical disorders such as diabetes.

Some components of psychoeducation can be found in every treatment approach. Table 11 identifies key elements of psychoeducational programs, with an emphasis on empirically based findings as to effective strategies that should be incorporated into treatment. However, psychoeducation alone has not been found to be effective in actually improving key treatment outcomes, such as increasing medication compliance or reducing hospitalizations. Imparting information and increasing the patient's knowledge of the disorder and its treatment appear to have limited positive effects if not combined with more specific strategies (Mueser, Corrigan, Hilton, Tanzman, Schaub, Gingerich, et al., 2002).

In a comprehensive review of psychoeducational treatment strategies for serious mental illness, including both schizophrenia and bipolar disorder, Mueser et al. (2002) analyzed 40 randomized controlled trials evaluating the evidence that a broad set of strategies – termed "illness management" and defined as " professional-based interventions designed to help people collaborate with professionals in the treatment of their mental illness, reduce their susceptibility to relapses, and cope more effectively with their symptoms" (p. 1273) – are effective in improving treatment outcomes. Mueser et al. (2002) specifically reviewed five types of approaches: broad-based psychoeducation, medication-focused programs, relapse prevention, coping skills training, and cognitive-behavioral treatment of psychotic symptoms.

The key finding for practitioners in the review by Mueser and colleagues is that broad-based psychoeducational strategies that focused on providing information alone did not necessarily improve treatment outcomes. For example, psychoeducational programs that provided information about medication, side effects, and strategies for managing side effects, while enhancing patient's knowledge about medication, did not necessarily improve their *actual* medication compliance.

Effective medication adherence strategies

Effective strategies for improving medication compliance involved two key components: (1) behavioral tailoring in which the patient is provided with specific and concrete strategies for incorporating medication into his or her daily routine; and (2) motivational interviewing which focuses on addressing a patient's concerns about medication. Psychoeducational programs focusing on specific strategies such as coping skills training, relapse prevention, and cognitive-behavioral treatment of psychotic symptoms were all found to be effective.

The rationale for applying a psychoeducational approach to bipolar disorder is that this disorder is most often a chronic episodic illness, in which new episodes can be linked to stressful environmental events (Johnson & Leahy, 2004). Successful management of the illness involves recognition of the need for continued treatment, including medication, which often has unwanted and unpleasant side effects even when the person is feeling relatively well. This is highly counterintuitive to say the least! Secondly, identification of stressors and the development of coping skills can mitigate the severity of future episodes.

A recent study by Colom, Vieta, and Martinez-Arán (2003) demonstrated the value of group psychoeducation with bipolar I disorder as compared to nondirective group meetings. The psychoeducational treatment focused on

Table 11
Key Elements of Effective Psychoeducational Programs

- Recognize the "readiness" of the patient/family to accept treatment and modify your approach accordingly, e.g., tailor information as specifically as possible to the patient's and family's concerns.

- Emphasize a collaborative approach, helping patients and family members become actively engaged in treatment.

- Enhance medication compliance by focusing on identifying specific beliefs and concerns that might interfere with treatment and developing concrete, specific behavioral strategies for daily compliance.

- Help patients monitor their activity and sleep levels and encourage a regular schedule.

- Help patients develop effective self-management skills, including:
  - managing stressors effectively
  - identifying warning signs of new episodes
  - developing specific coping skills, and
  - formulating a relapse plan

increasing awareness of the disorder, enhancing medication compliance, helping to stabilize social rhythms, and detecting symptoms of recurrence.

2.3   The Interpersonal and Social Rhythm Hypothesis: Social Rhythm Disruption as a Potential Catalyst for Bipolar Episodes

A second theoretical approach to the conceptualization and treatment of bipolar disorder, the Interpersonal and Social Rhythm Therapy (IPSRT) developed by Frank, Swartz, and Kupfer (2000) has focused on the episodic and cyclical nature of the illness. Interpersonal Psychotherapy (IPT) was originally developed and demonstrated to be effective in the treatment of depression. Based upon earlier work reviewing the relationship between bipolar disorder and circadian rhythm disturbances (Goodwin & Jamison, 1990), Frank and others hypothesized that appropriate mood regulation in patients with bipolar disorder is in part a function of their social rhythms, including levels of stimulation and daily activity. Several researchers have argued that the primary biological pathway to the disorder is through disruptions in the individuals' circadian rhythms, and that individuals with bipolar disorder are especially sensitive to these disruptions (Frank et al., 2000; Lam, Jones, Hayward, & Bright, 1999). Malkoff-Schwartz, Frank, and Anderson (1998) studied the degree to which social routine or rhythm disruption acts as a catalyst for manic and depressive bipolar episodes. The concept espoused is that social routines such as sleeping, eating, and periods of activity help to "entrain" circadian rhythms (Malhoff-Schwartz et al., 1998, p. 702). The greater the disruption in regular activity, the more likely it is that patients with bipolar disorder will become dysregulated and detached from their normal circadian rhythms.

Key elements of effective psychoeducational programs

Interpersonal and
social rhythm (IPSRT)
hypothesis

Table 12

Key Objectives of Interpersonal and Social Rhythm Therapy (Adapted from Frank et al., 1999)

- Helping patients recognize the relationship between mood and life events
- Helping patients manage stressful life events
- Assisting patients in stabilizing disrupted social rhythms
- Addressing medication noncompliance
- Focusing on the impact of the illness in terms of loss, grief over lost roles, and role transitions
- Addressing interpersonal difficulties and deficits in social skills

These investigators reported that social routine disrupting (Frank, Hlastala, Ritenour, Houck, Tu, Monk, et al., 1997) events over an 8-week pre-onset period were strongly associated with the onset of mania. For individuals with this vulnerability, instability in circadian rhythms is not self-correcting as it is in nonvulnerable populations. Disruptions can lead to increasing desynchronization or disentrainment of the sleep/wake cycle, which then leads to somatic symptoms and eventually the onset of a manic or depressive episode (Ehlers, Frank, & Kupfer, 1988; Frank et al., 1997; Frank, Swartz, Mallinger, Thase, Weaver, & Kupfer, 1999). The goal of IPSRT is to assist patients in stabilizing their social and interpersonal routines and to avoid or minimize potentially disrupting events or circumstances likely to impact their stability. Table 12 lists some of the key objectives outlined in this therapy that are based on the model as described above.

2.4   Family-Based Treatment Approaches

Key objectives for
interpersonal and
social rhythm (IPSRT)

Family-based treatment approaches for bipolar disorder evolved from earlier findings as to the role of negative expressed emotion (EE) in families of schizophrenics in producing higher levels of relapse and rehospitalization (Miklowitz, 2004). Family-based treatment of bipolar disorder emphasizes psychoeducation, communication skills training, and developing problem-solving skills among family members in order to reduce the level of conflict and distress in the family. Six major objectives of family-focused treatment

Key objectives
for family-
based treatment
approaches

Table 13

Key Objectives in Family-Focused Treatment (Miklowitz, 2002)

- Help patient and family members integrate experiences with bipolar disorder
- Assist patient/family members in accepting vulnerability to future episodes.
- Assist patient/family members in accepting ongoing need for medication.
- Help patient/family members differentiate between effects of bipolar disorder and patient's personality.
- Assist patient/family members in recognizing and coping with stressful events (likely to trigger new episodes).
- Help family reestablish functional relationships.

are summarized in Table 13. The main assumption underlying this approach is that reducing stress in the family environment can delay, minimize, or possibly prevent recurrences of bipolar disorder. Family-focused treatment recognizes the role of underlying biological/genetic vulnerability to the disorder and proposes a stress-vulnerability model that accounts for both environmental and innate biological factors.

2.5 Cognitive-Behavioral Treatment Approaches

Cognitive-behavioral therapy has already demonstrated efficacy in the treatment of depression. A recent review of psychosocial interventions with bipolar disorder concluded that, "In summary, individual CBT [cognitive behavioral therapy] appears to be the most broadly effective of bipolar psychosocial interventions in both open and controlled trials" (Zaretsky, 2003, p. 85) . There are several different approaches to cognitive behavior therapy for bipolar disorder that have been studied in randomized trials. At least three approaches that will be reviewed below have well-developed treatment protocols that are currently available.

2.5.1 Basco and Rush Cognitive-Behavioral Treatment of Bipolar Disorder

Basco and Rush (1996) developed the first comprehensive cognitive-behavioral treatment manual specifically for the treatment of bipolar disorder. The authors identify critical problems in the pharmacological management of bipolar disorder, namely the lack of medication compliance and the presence of subsyndromal symptoms of mania and depression even when patients are fully compliant. The argument is made that long-term management with a mood stabilizer must be supplemented with psychosocial treatment to enhance medication compliance and assist patients in identifying psychosocial stressors that may precipitate new episodes of the illness.

Cognitive behavioral approaches

The treatment model assumes that there is a reciprocal relationship between thoughts, perceptions, feelings, and behaviors that can contribute to the acceleration of prodromal symptoms into full episodes of illness. This "downward spiral" or "vicious cycle" is produced by the interaction of early changes in mood, thinking (reckless optimism, grandiosity, poor judgment), and behavior (risk-taking behaviors, sleep, appetite, activity level) that can further impair functioning, resulting in a worsening slide into depression and mania. If we also take into account the role of social support and interpersonal relationships, we can readily see how impaired functioning affects support systems and leads to additional stress and distress.

The "downward spiral"

Basco and Rush identify several primary treatment targets that focus on intervening at key points in this cycle of early mood symptoms. Medication can address biological vulnerabilities in terms of preventing and controlling acute symptoms of mania and depression but cannot target these other potentially critical intervention points in terms of altering changes in thinking,

Table 14
Key Treatment Objectives for Cognitive-Behavioral Treatment of Bipolar Disorder
(Basco & Rush, 1996)

- Educate patients about the disorder, treatment approaches, and common problems associated with bipolar disorder.
- Teach patients to monitor mood and associated symptoms methodically.
- Promote medication compliance.
- Develop cognitive and behavioral skills for ameliorating the cognitive, affective and behavioral changes associated with manic and depressive episodes.
- Help patients develop more effective coping and problem solving strategies to reduce stress.

changes in behavior, psychosocial functioning, and stress-related disruptions of sleep and routines. This is a comprehensive pragmatic treatment approach which attempts to develop systematic skills in mood monitoring, identifying stressors, identifying early warning signs, and developing problem solving and coping skills (see Table 14).

2.5.2   Lam, Jones, Hayward, and Bright (1999): Identifying Prodromes of Illness

Another group of cognitive-behavioral therapists (Lam, Jones, Hayward, & Bright 1999; Lam & Wong, 1997; Lam, Wong, & Sham, 2001) have proposed a "holistic" diathesis-stress model for bipolar disorder that highlights the role of prodrome identification (or identification of early warning signs of illness) and the development of coping strategies as key treatment components. As discussed earlier, the diathesis stress model posits a dual role for both biological and social-psychological factors in the production of episodes of illness. An inherent biological vulnerability is coupled with psychological and social factors such as stressful events, disruptions in circadian rhythms, and lack

Stress-vulnerability
model adapted from
Lam et al. (1999)

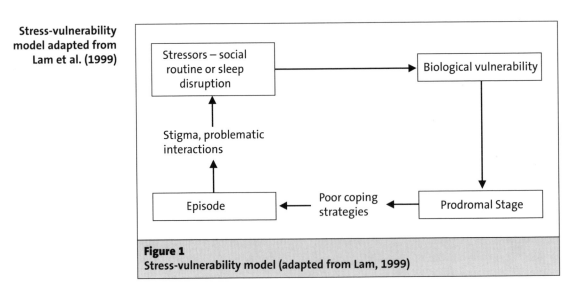

Figure 1
Stress-vulnerability model (adapted from Lam, 1999)

Key objectives in
Lam's model

Table 15
**Key Treatment Objectives of Cognitive-Behavioral Therapy for Bipolar Disorder
(Adapted from Lam et al., 1999)**

- Development of a collaborative working relationship
- Psychoeducation on the diathesis-stress model with a focus on helping patients learn problem-solving skills to manage stress
- Developing specific cognitive-behavioral skills for coping with prodromes, including monitoring for prodromes, developing coping strategies, and altering behavior
- Assisting patients in maintaining stable routines and getting adequate amounts of sleep
- Helping patients address long-term vulnerabilities (such as excessive goal-driven behavior) to reduce future episodes

regularity of social routines, and as a result produces new episodes of illness. In Lam's model, specifically, the relative effectiveness of the individual's coping strategies in the prodromal phase of the illness is viewed as an important determinant of acceleration into an acute episode. This specific cognitive-behavioral model emphasizes the primary role of identification of prodromes of illness and the development of coping strategies as key components in the treatment of bipolar disorder, in addition to other factors such as psychoeducation and maintaining social rhythms (see Figure 1).

This treatment model contains a few critical assumptions: (1) that with specific training, patients are able to detect prodromal signs of illness effectively; (2) that a skills-based approach can help patients develop more effective coping strategies; and (3) that more effective coping strategies will be prophylactic against the development of severe manic and depressive episodes.

2.5.3   Other Cognitive Behavioral Treatment Strategies with Bipolar Disorder

Other cognitive-
behavioral
approaches

As indicated earlier, cognitive-behavioral therapies have demonstrated effectiveness for major depressive episodes (Barlow, 2001; Beck et al., 1979; Lambert, 2004). Cognitive-behavioral therapy targets the belief systems regarding self, world, and other that make the patient vulnerable to depression. (Beck et al., 1979). The assumption is that patients are vulnerable to depressive episodes in part because of a bias in their information processing system that causes them to misconstrue or misinterpret events in a negative direction. Thoughts, feeling, and behavior are viewed as having a reciprocal relationship such that, for example, negative thinking ("I'm incompetent – I won't be able to do this") might lead to changes in behavior (giving up, not trying, avoiding tasks, isolating, withdrawing) which can then lead to an increasing sense of depression and even lowered self-esteem. This in turn might lead to further self-critical thoughts ("What a loser I am, I couldn't even do this simple task"), increasing immobility and a lowered mood.

Newman, Leahy, Beck, Reilly-Harrington, and Gyulai, (2002) have developed a cognitive treatment model for bipolar disorder that highlights the central role of cognitive factors in the production of new bipolar episodes. Newman et al. (2002) propose that, in addition to biological vulnerabilities, cognitive factors (e.g., distortions in the patient's perceptions, information processing, belief systems, and judgment) act as primary contributors to the development of continuing episodes of illness. The treatment aims to modify the patient's beliefs, especially long-standing schema (fundamental beliefs that channel the patient's cognitive processing of events) that increase the patient's vulnerability to manic and depressive episodes. The assumption is that modification of these cognitive vulnerabilities can fortify the patient against the continuing vicious cycle of manic and depressive episodes by developing more effective coping and problemsolving abilities and reducing vulnerability to stress. In addition, this treatment approach utilizes a range of behavioral interventions to assist patients in delaying impulsive actions in the manic and hypomanic phases (see Table 16).

Key objectives in the Newman et al. (2002) model

Table 16
Key Treatment Objectives of the Cognitive-Behavioral Treatment Model (adapted from Newman et al., 2002)

- Modify maladaptive beliefs or cognitive vulnerabilities that predispose patients to severe episodes of depression and mania.

- For mania/hypomania:
  1. Address maladaptive perceptions, judgment, and behaviors.
  2. Moderate hypomanic/manic thinking by counterbalancing overly positive thoughts and beliefs.
  3. Moderate impulsivity and recklessness by encouraging delaying behaviors and tactics.
  4. Help the patient modulate affect.
  5. Assist patients in reducing disorganization and distractibility.

- For depression
  1. Address maladaptive perceptions, judgment, and behaviors.
  2. Counteract hopelessness and demoralization.
  3. Address suicidal beliefs.
  4. Increase mastery and pleasure.
  5. Teach problem-solving skills.
  6. Develop social support systems.

3

Diagnosis and Treatment Indications

This chapter provides advice on treatment indications (i.e., how to determine the most appropriate treatment), including a decision tree for evaluating the best treatment options/settings.

One of the major goals of this book is to expand the use of evidence-based structured outpatient treatment with bipolar disorder by giving the practitioner access to effective treatment tools. However, not every practitioner will want to take on the responsibility of treating patients with bipolar disorder in a private practice setting. Patients with bipolar disorder provide significant clinical challenges, often presenting with complex problems and comorbid psychiatric and substance abuse disorders. However, because of the combination of effective treatments that are now available and the lack of clinical resources available to patients, especially for ongoing maintenance treatment in outpatient and clinic settings, treatment of this disorder can be extremely rewarding and gratifying.

Certain patients cannot be properly treated in this setting and present too serious a risk to be appropriately managed. How will you decide whether or not you should consider treating an individual with bipolar disorder? Your decision-making process should consider the overall stability of the patient, the degree to which they present with high-risk symptoms, and their willingness to comply with psychiatric and psychological treatment regimens. Table 17 describes some of the key factors to be considered.

Table 17
Determining if the Patient is Appropriate for an Outpatient Private Practice or Clinic Setting

- Has the patient agreed to take a mood stabilizer and is the patient compliant with treatment?
- Is there a pattern of recent instability suggesting that standard outpatient treatment will not be sufficient for the patient to remain stable?
- Does the patient have sufficient social supports available at this point?
- Is the patient too acutely ill to benefit from outpatient care at this stage (e.g., multiple hospitalizations or emergency room visits in the past month)
- Does the patient present an acute suicide risk that cannot be managed in outpatient care?
- Will the patient be able to comply with the requirements of outpatient treatment in terms of showing up for regularly scheduled appointments?
- Is the patient sufficiently motivated to commit to a course of outpatient treatment?

While there is no absolute empirical basis for making treatment recommendations as to which of the four psychosocial treatment strategies described in Chapters 2 and 3 is likely to be preferred as a first line treatment, there are a number of considerations that can guide the practitioner in making reasonable choices based upon the data available. This guide takes a "best practices" approach, attempting to synthesize empirical data and expert knowledge as well as clinical experience. In a recent review of psychosocial interventions for bipolar disorder, Zaretsky (2003) concludes as follows:

"Because bipolar disorder is a complex illness characterized by different phases of illness, there are many different targets for treatment. Treatment of acute episodes is likely best accomplished by pharmacotherapy ... There is evidence from studies reviewed that different interventions have different effects on depression and mania. Psychoeducational interventions appear to improve medication compliance and should be considered early in the course of illness. Treatment interventions that focus primarily on helping patients identify early prodromes of relapse in order to take proactive steps have also been shown to be effective ... Such interventions should be considered after medication adherence has been adequately addressed." (Zaretsky, 2003, p. 85)

There are a number of considerations suggested here that indicate possible treatment choices based on:

1. Acuity of the presentation in terms of type of current presenting symptoms and risk factors
2. Phase of illness (primarily hypomanic, manic, depressive or mixed)
3. Course of the illness

3.1   Decision Tree for Determining Optimal Treatments

Decision tree for choice of treatment

As noted above, empirical data is lacking to make definitive statements as to optimal treatments. However, there is a menu of reasonable choices that should be considered, based upon several factors that should be assessed in the initial interviews. In addition to a standard initial assessment incorporating some of the features discussed in Chapter 1, your initial interviews should serve to address the key items in Table 18.

The information obtained will enable the therapist to draw conclusions concerning the severity, particular phase, and general course of the illness and develop a menu of the most appropriate clinical treatment options.

3.2   Treatment Options

3.2.1   Treatment Options for Young Adult

Treatment options: Young adult recently hospitalized

For example, treatment options for a young adult with a recent hospitalization for a first episode might focus on a cluster of symptoms involving denial of illness, medication nonadherence, and high levels of family-related conflict.

Table 18:
Additional Helpful Information to be Developed in Initial Interviews

1. Acuity of current presentation in terms of type of current presenting symptoms and risk factors:
   a) Level of suicidal risk
   b) Degree of medication compliance
   c) Impairments in coping and social skills
   d) Currently psychotic or with poor reality testing
   e) Current substance misuse
   f) Degree of hopelessness and demoralization
   g) Impairments in current functioning
   h) Impairments in current judgment
   i) Presence of other high risk factors/behaviors

2. The phase of illness (current episode hypomanic, manic or depressed):
   a) Acute manic state
   b) Acute depressive state
   c) Hypomanic
   d) Mixed
   e) Degree of interepisode recovery
   f) Highest level of functioning
   g) Presence of subsyndromal dysthmia and depression

3. The course of the illness:
   a) Age of patient
   b) Course of the disorder to date

4. Environmental factors
   a) Interpersonal, family, and social stressors
   b) Interpersonal, family, and social supports
   c) Job, career, school-related problems
   d) Goals and aspirations
   e) Ability to manage without structured, supervised living situation

5. Other social and psychological factors
   a) Family/significant other engagement
   b) Degree of medication compliance
   c) Degree of acceptance/denial of illness
   d) Degree of overall readiness and engagement in treatment
   e) Willingness to accept help in therapeutic relationship

First-line treatment options are likely to include psychoeducation, focus on engagement and normalizing, motivational interviewing to enhance medication adherence, and family-focused treatment.

3.2.2   Treatment Options for High Risk Presentation

For an individual with a higher-risk presentation, including episode features such as a recent hospitalization with the patient presenting as seriously hypomanic or depressed, with suicidal ideation/past behavior, high-risk hypomanic behaviors (impulsive risk-taking, pleasure-seeking, poor judgment) or medication nonadherence, possible interventions might include a pharmacological assessment and intervention, psychotherapy targeting hopelessness and demoralization, assisting the patient in utilizing "delay tactics" and behavioral strategies limiting overactivity and stimulation to contain impulsive behaviors, and motivational interviewing to enhance medication adherence.

3.2.3   Treatment Options for Repeated Episodes of Mania/ Hypomania (see the case of Bill in Section 4.1.5)

Treatment options: Repeated hospitalizations

For an individual with a repeated history of manic episodes with psychotic features or hypomanic episodes, denial of illness, or unable to detect prodromes who is medication compliant, possible interventions might include pharmacological interventions, psychoeducation, focus on monitoring prodromes of mania, and developing behaviorally oriented coping plans triggered by early warning signs.

3.2.4   Treatment Options for Persistent Subsyndromal Depression and Dysthmia (see the case of Tanya in Section 4.4.2)

Treatment options: Persistent subsyndromal depression

For an individual with bipolar episode features including poor interepisode recovery with significant subsyndromal depression or dysthmia, or a higher functioning patient who accepts a chronically low level of functioning and appears hopeless and demoralized, possible interventions might include behavioral interventions to activate the patient, schema-based work to identify long-term self-concept distortions, and cognitive interventions to combat hopelessness.

Treatment

4.1 Methods of Treatment

4.1.1 Biological Approaches to Treatment of Bipolar Disorder

There are several sets of best practices or consensus guidelines for the development of medication treatment protocols for bipolar disorder. The reader will want to reference at least the following sets of guidelines: the Texas Medication Algorithm Project (TMAP) Guidelines (Suppes, Swann, Dennehy, Habermacher, Mason, Crismon, et al., 2001), Sachs and colleagues, summary of consensus guidelines (Sachs, Printz, Kahn, Carpenter, & Docherty, 2000), APA *Practice guidelines for the treatment of psychiatric disorders* (APA, 2004), and Section 13.8, Mood Disorders: Treatment of Bipolar Disorders in *Kaplan & Sadock's comprehensive textbook of psychiatry*, 8th Edition (2005). Unfortunately, due to rapid changes in research and the development of new medications, guidelines for best practices must be continually updated. The brief review presented here for suggested use of medications in bipolar disorder is for general information and didactic purposes only and is not intended to be relied upon as an up-to-date treatment protocol for psychiatric medication management.

Sachs et al. (2000) developed a set of consensus or best practice guidelines based upon a national survey of 65 experts. The key recommendations include the use of a mood stabilizer in all phases of treatment of the disorder. Divalproex and lithium were the top-rated choices (at the time of the survey) for monotherapy with a mood stabilizer. Carbamazepine, especially for mania, and lamotrigine, especially for depression, were ranked as the two leading alternative mood stabilizers. For acute mania with psychosis, an atypical antipsychotic was added as the mood stabilizer as a first-line option. Atypical antipsychotics were always preferred over older conventional antipsychotics because of their more favorable side effect profile. The survey results supported the use of monotherapy with a mood stabilizer for mild depression, while severe depression was viewed as best treated with a mood stabilizer plus an antidepressant. Bupropion and selective serotonin reuptake inhibitors (SSRIs) were favored over older tricyclic antidepressants again, because of superior side effect profiles. In this survey, experts recommended that antidepressants be tapered in 2–6 months (significantly different than recommendations in the treatment of depression). For augmentation strategies when patients were not responding to a mood stabilizer plus an antidepressant after an appropriate trial, the survey experts recommended adding lithium. Finally, for presenta-

Pharmacological treatment: Best practice guidelines

tions with either mania or depression with rapid cycling, a mood stabilizer alone, preferably divalproex, was recommended.

Pharmacological treatment: Recent reviews

In a 2004 update, Sachs (2004) presented a summary of the quality of evidence for psychotropics used with bipolar disorder, assigning a rating of Category "A" for double-blind placebo-controlled trials with adequate samples to the following pharmacological strategies:

- **For acute mania/mixed:** Lithium, divalproex, carbamazepine, haloperidol, aripiprazole, olanzapine, risperdone, quetiapine
- **For acute bipolar depression:** Lamotrigine, olanzapine, quetiapine
- **For rapid cycling:** Lamotrigine
- **For prophylaxis (mood stabilizer):** Lithium, divalproex, lamotrigine, aripiprazole

Post and Altshuler (in Sadock & Sadock, 2005) note that while lithium remains the gold standard of mood stabilizers in terms of its effectiveness in preventing suicide, new prescriptions for valproic acid (Depakene) and divalproex (Depakote) have superseded prescriptions for lithium since the mid-1990s. Additional mood stabilizers including carbamazepine (Tegretol), and lamotrigine (Lamictal) have been increasingly recognized as alternatives to lithium. These authors also note that oxcarbazepine (Trileptal), levetiracetam (Keppra), and zonisamide (Zonegram) represent promising third-generation mood stabilizers still under study. Finally, Post and Altshuler conclude "There are imprecise guidelines for initially choosing among these agents, and guidelines are completely lacking for their use in dual or complex therapy, which is increasingly necessary to achieve remission and mood stability in bipolar illness .... Precisely defining when and how and in what combination these treatments and adjuncts are used remains a considerable clinical challenge that is in need of systematic clinical study" (page 1663).

The following summary of pharmacological approaches to bipolar disorder is adapted from recommendations in the Post and Altshuler chapter in the *Comprehensive Textbook of Psychiatry* 8th Edition (2005):

Pharmacological treatment: Acute mania

- **For treatment of acute mania:** Lithium plus an atypical antipsychotic or a high-potency benzodiazepine including clonazepam (Klonopin) or lorazepam (Ativan) is indicated. For cases presenting with nonresponse to lithium, dysphoric mania, or rapid cycling, valproate is recommended. Carbamazepine is considered a third alternative for lithium nonresponders. The following atypical antipsychotics have all demonstrated antimanic properties and are listed by Post and Altshuler in order based upon the strength of data available at the time of publication: clozapine (Clozaril), risperidone (Risperdal), olanzapine (Zyprexa), quetiapine (Seroquel), ziprasidone (Geodon), and aripipazole (Abilify).

Pharmacological treatment: Bipolar depression

- **For acute treatment of bipolar depression:** Lithium, lamotrigine, and carbamazepine have documented antidepressant effects. The current consensus, as of the Post and Altshuler review, suggests combining an antidepressant with a mood stabilizer as a first line of treatment for bipolar depression. Use of an SSRI antidepressant with bupropion and venlafaxine appears to be the preferred first-line treatment in addition to a mood stabilizer.

- **Maintenance treatment of bipolar disorder:** The first line of treatment for this disorder in any phase is ongoing treatment with a mood stabilizer. Lithium is still a first choice for mood stabilizer due to its robust long-term efficacy data and its documented suicide prevention effects. The authors recommend preventive treatment after a single manic episode, especially if there is a family history of bipolar disorder. Due to low response rates (less than 50%), for nonresponders and individuals unable to tolerate the side effects of lithium, other mood stabilizers including carbamazepine, valproic acid, and lamotrigine may be considered. Although some of the atypical antipsychotics have demonstrated antimanic efficacy and possible effects on depression, use of these compounds for long-term prophylaxis must take into account a number of serious side effects, including, among others, weight gain and risk of diabetes.

Pharmacological treatment: Maintenance

Once stabilization is obtained a decision will need to be made regarding what medications will be required and what should be discontinued to avoid relapse or the delayed onset of serious side effects. Again, this may require the shifting of various medications depending on the patient's reaction to the drug regimen changes. In summary, a variety of strategies might be explored before the best efficacy-to-side-effect profile is found, and a stable maintenance program is established. All this must be accomplished in the context of dealing with a disturbed individual, who more often than not continues to be unstable and may even be noncompliant with the treatment program.

Below is a list of some of the more common agents in use today in the treatment of bipolar disorder. The focus here will be on the medications that are considered to have specific mood stabilizing properties:

Lithium carbonate has been the mainstay for the treatment of acute mania and its subsequent prevention. The action of this drug is slow and in the case of an acute episode it is often combined initially with an atypical antipsychotic or a mood stabilizing anticonvulsant. Lithium seems to work more effectively with patients who present with euphoria rather than a more dysphoric manic state.

List of common medications for treating bipolar disorder

Divalproex (Depakote) is a mood stabilizer often administered in addition to lithium carbonate, because it has a quick response. Divalproex tends to have a higher frequency of response in patients with typical manic symptoms rather than schizoaffective symptoms. Also, many individuals with rapid cycling or dysphoric mania tend to respond better to this drug than to lithium.

Carbamazepine (Tegretol) is another mood stabilizer that is often considered for patients who do not respond to Lithium. The therapeutic range and side-effect profile for this drug is variable across patients, so dosage must be individualized carefully.

Lamotrigine (Lamictal), which is effective as an acute and prophylactic antidepressant agent, is emerging as a possible mood stabilizer and as a first-line treatment in bipolar depression along with an antidepressant. Slow titration and dosing strategies are critical in that a severe life threatening rash (Stevens-Johnson syndrome) can develop.

Clonazepam (Klonopin) and **Lorazepam** (Ativan), two high-potency benzodiazepines, are often used as an adjunctive treatment for patients with acute manic agitation, insomnia, dysphoria, and panic. They are considered ideal companion medications for mood stabilizers, because of relatively few side effects. Long-term use of this drug class, however, may be problematic.

Virtually all of the **atypical antipsychotics** have proven effective in the treatment of mania, particularly in combination with mood stabilizers, and they have fewer side effects than the typical psychotics, which makes them more attractive as adjunctive medications. Some do result in weight gain, which eventually could lead to cardiovascular complications or other medical problems associated with obesity. **Clozapine** is reported to be highly effective in patients characterized by dysphoric mania and rapid cycling. **Risperidone** has proven to be effective in acute mania. Patients on low doses, however, tend to gain weight. **Olanzapine** (Zyprexa) has proven to be effective with some treatment refractory patients. It is well tolerated, except for the problem of serious weight gain. **Quetiapine** (Seroquel) is a newer drug that is effective as a single medication or as an adjunct to mood stabilizers. This medication also may be an effective antidepressant. **Zisprasidone** (Geodon) is an atypical antipsychotic that does not result in weight gain. There is also some suggestion that Zisprasidone may have antidepressant properties, as well.

4.1.2 Psychosocial Approaches to Treatment of Bipolar Disorder: General Remarks

Although the primary treatment for bipolar disorder continues to be the use of mood stabilizing medication, there has recently been renewed interest in psychosocial treatment approaches. While there are variations in different therapy models, successful treatments share several common features that address both biological/genetic factors as well as the need to manage stress and maintain a regular social routine. For example, patients are taught about the role of daily routines and regular sleep/wake cycles; work with the therapist to establish regular routines; learn to identify prodromal signs and symptoms by monitoring mood and activity/stimulation levels; and attempt to resolve stressful events in their lives and develop specific coping strategies to avert relapse (Frank et al., 2000; Lam et al., 2003; Jones, Hayward, & Bright, 1999; Scott, 2001). In a number of studies, cognitive-behavioral treatment has demonstrated significant promise in stabilizing mood and decreasing relapses and recidivism (Huxley, Parikh, & Baldessarini, 2000; Lam et al., 1999; Perry, Tarrier, Morriss, McCarthy, & Limb, 1999; Scott, Garland, & Moorhead, 2001). For example, Lam, Watkins, Hayward, Bright, Wright, Kerr, et al. (2003), utilizing random assignment with over 100 patients, demonstrated that a specialized cognitive-behavioral treatment including monitoring of prodromes, development of specific coping strategies, and promoting social rhythm stability was associated with significantly fewer bipolar episodes, fewer days in a bipolar episode, and fewer hospital admissions in the 12 months under study.

The Use of Active, Directive, Structured Therapy

Use of active, directive and structured therapy

There is no empirical evidence that unstructured, nondirective psychosocial treatments are effective in treating bipolar disorder. On the contrary, every effective treatment protocol presented in the literature for bipolar disorder requires a highly organized, directive, and structured approach. Consistent

Table 19:
Elements of Evidence-Based Treatment of Bipolar Disorder

- Educate patients and family members about the illness (Mueser et al., 2002)
- Where appropriate, treat family members or significant others in order to reduce conflict and negative expressed emotion in the family and develop support systems (Miklowitz & Alloy, 1999; Miklowitz, George, Richards, Simoneau, & Suddath, 2003; Miklowitz, Goldstein, Nuechterlein, Snyder, & Minz, 1988)
- Focus on improving treatment/medication adherence (Goodwin & Jamison, 1990)
- Teach patients to routinely monitor mood and activity state/level of stimulation (Frank et al., 1997, 2000)
- Assist patients in detecting prodromes of illness including mood and activity level changes (Lam et al., 1999)
- Modify maladaptive beliefs – or cognitive vulnerabilities that predispose patients to severe episodes of depression and mania (Newman, Leahy, Beck, Reilly-Harrington, & Gyulai, 2002)
- Address maladaptive perceptions, judgment, and behaviors
- Assist patients in problem-solving and coping strategies to reduce the impact of aversive life events that precipitate syndromal or subsyndromal mood swings (Lam et al., 1999)
- Assist patients in stabilizing lifestyle and social routines (Frank et al., 2000)
- Develop coping plans to prevent or minimize relapses (Basco & Rush, 1996; Lam et al., 1999).
- Develop a relapse prevention plan

with the spirit of most active, directive treatments (including cognitive-behavioral therapy), we present here a series of treatment strategies that are highly structured, agenda-driven, and skill focused. The intent is to teach patients a core set of skills that have a strong evidence base in terms of their effectiveness with bipolar depression and mania. This is consistent with the model of illness management strategies presented in Mueser et al. (2002) The primary goals of an integrated, evidence-based treatment program are presented in Table 19.

4.1.3 Overall Structure and Course of Therapy

The overall course of therapy can be conceptualized in three distinct phases. The *initial phase* involves assessment and development of treatment goals, and orientation of the patient(s) to the unique strategies employed in this structured treatment program. This usually takes two or three sessions, but there is overlap with the aims of the *middle phase*, which places substantial focus on the development of skills. The number of sessions can vary as a function of many factors, such as severity and complexity of the patient's disorder, allocation of time span for therapy determined by institutional policies, patient's progress in therapy, etc. Even when working within the framework of a brief therapy model oriented to skills acquisition, bipolar disorders typically require a substantial amount of clinical contact time. Presently, we recommend that at least 12–15 weekly sessions should be allotted to the skill acquisition phase, followed by four or five bimonthly sessions at a minimum. This sets the stage for the *final phase*, which focuses primarily on maintenance of gains and relapse prevention. This involves monthly sessions to review progress and make any adjustments required to minimize relapse and recurrence of episodes. For many low functioning patients, who are in residential facilities, this can be a time to explore the possibility of educational or vocational training, job acquisition, changes in housing, improved transportation capabilities, or other adjustments leading towards social recovery. Positive changes in some of these areas often alleviate some of the environmental stresses that are likely to trigger the occurrence of episodes. A recent study by Lam and colleagues suggests that continuing maintenance treatment should be a first line choice (Lam, Hayward, Watkins, Wright, & Sham, 2005).

4.1.4   Initial Phase of Treatment: Orientation and Engagement

The Need for a Collaborative Approach

Need for a collaborative approach

Active engagement and collaboration with the patient is a primary key to success in treatment. Contrary to a stereotypical view of cognitive and behavioral approaches, the heart and soul of cognitive-behavioral therapy is the formation of a collaborative relationship between the therapist and patient. This overarching structure must be in place so that both the therapist and the patient can take an active role in understanding the problems that brought the individual to therapy, in defining the goals of therapy, in working to achieve those goals and in working through the termination. A collaborative model requires that the initial phase of treatment be devoted to engaging the patient and motivating him or her to continue in therapy. The model is one of active participation and self-management of the illness. Of necessity, a number of logistical and practical issues must be covered that comprise the major substance of this initial phase.

Improving Adherence to the Intervention and Reducing Attrition

Improving adherence to treatment

First, the patient population targeted by this treatment program, especially lower functioning patients seen in mental health clinic settings, frequently experience significant attendance problems, difficulty following through on assigned tasks, and attrition. This is especially true for individuals with bipolar disorder who have inherent, biologically based difficulties with self-regulation, maintaining structure and routines, and completing assigned tasks. With such patients the maintenance of a consistent, structured treatment program is likely to require weekly and periodic extra-treatment patient contacts, at least in the initial phase and in some instances during the entire course of therapy, in order to enhance engagement in treatment and adherence to the treatment regimen. In the initial weeks of therapy, patients should receive reminder calls

Use of telephone contacts

in the 24 hours before scheduled individual or group sessions. Personal calls greatly enhance a patient's motivation to continue in treatment, particularly during episodes of more serious depression and mania. Patients are usually grateful for these reminders, which help them maintain structure in their daily and weekly activities. Patients who miss sessions should routinely receive follow-up calls to review material scheduled to be covered in the session and to develop homework assignments. In most cases, patients appreciate the effort made by clinic staff to keep them informed and involved in the treatment program. Patients who miss more than one consecutive treatment session or those identified as at high risk for drop should receive calls directly from the individual therapist, or from group facilitators if group therapy is being employed. Other calls may be made by a project coordinator or other clinic personnel, including case managers. In some cases, a personal call to a patient has served as an important reassurance that treatment is important and that the therapist is concerned about their absence.

A useful strategy for emphasizing the importance of attendance from the start is to develop a formal contract with the patient that highlights their responsibility for attendance (see Appendix 2). After signing the contract, it is extremely useful to discuss what some of the barriers to attendance might be, and how the patient might deal with these in order to maintain a high level of attendance.

Developing an Expectation of Active Participation

A second goal in the initial phase of treatment is to develop active participation and an expectation that the patient will be a problem-solver and will be required to follow through on a number of tasks including: attending treatment sessions, even though they may be feeling hopeless and demoralized (or overly optimistic and dismissive of treatment), ongoing monitoring of symptoms, and completing homework assignments. This requires a high level of active individual patient and/or group participation. The goal is to create a collaborative environment in which individual patients or group members participate actively in a variety of exercises in order to acquire key skills.

Informing Patients About the Therapy Model

Thirdly, it is important to help patients understand the theoretical basis for the therapy and how this will be applied in weekly sessions. Although their functioning may be low, almost all patients can comprehend a straight-forward explanation of a skills-based treatment program. If at all possible, it is very effective to use information about problems or complaints the patient has talked about initially as concrete illustrations of how the model works. This more personalized approach facilitates understanding of the model. A reading assignment explaining the model and rationale in lay language is often a good initial home practice assignment. It is important to be sure that the patient has some understanding of the basics of the model and how this type of therapy might be similar to or different from other therapy experiences they have had. The patient needs to understand from the outset that the therapy is highly structured and collaborative in nature. And so, a detailed explanation of what will transpire in therapy, accompanied by the rationale for how this will be helpful, should occur fairly early in the initial phase of treatment. Patients need to appreciate that they will be expected to be active participants in the process and that they will have to complete home practice assignments to help them learn how to deal with life events and their consequent mood swings. There are a number of excellent descriptions of the underlying stress vulnerability models used in structured treatment approaches with bipolar disorder (Goodwin & Jamison, 1990; Basco & Rush, 1996; Lam et al., 1999; Goldstein & Miklowitz, 1994). We use a model adapted from Basco and Rush (1996) that emphasizes the reciprocal relationship among thoughts, emotions, behaviors, and physi-

Explaining the model to patients

ological processes. Once the patient becomes familiar with this model, some variation of the following discussion might be appropriate:

"You mentioned that your main problem is to get control over these terrible mood swings you're having. It's pretty hard to just change how you're feeling directly, but we can work on some of the other things that affect how you're feeling. Even though we can't work on the feelings directly, we still have these two areas, thoughts and behaviors, that we can work on to make you feel better. This is good because we can help you learn to change how you look at things, which can make you feel better, and we also can help you learn to do things that will make you feel better."

Eliciting Target Complaints and Formulating Treatment Goals

Formulating initial treatment goals

A fourth important feature in the initial phase is to elicit target complaints from the patient, and then work collaboratively with the patient to formulate one or more of these complaints into initial treatment goals. Treatment goals should reflect a well-defined plan for change, not a general complaint or ill-defined problem; be relevant to a particular problem the patient has raised; and, be framed so that it has specific components that are measurable.

Assuring that meaningful personal goals are included

Treatment goals should be personally meaningful to the patient. Too often, clinicians focus primarily on a reduction in psychiatric symptoms as a primary goal of treatment. In our experience, it is important to develop the "big picture" in terms of the patient's values, interests, and objectives in life in order to incorporate these into meaningful treatment goals that reflect level of functioning. While "becoming less depressed" is an important symptomatic goal, it is hardly motivating in terms of a meaningful life goal. It is useful to take a recovery-based approach in which patients are encouraged to identify (and eventually pursue) truly meaningful life goals that will provide sufficient motivation to endure a difficult course of treatment, often including unpleasant side effects from medication. Because patients often begin treatment in a demoralized and hopeless state, the clinician's role is to help them develop an expectation of success in achieving important life goals and ambitions, despite a history of severe and recurrent episodes of illness in the past.

Making treatment goals concrete and specific

Treatment goals should be as concrete and specific as possible. For example, whenever a patient lists "high self-esteem" as a goal, we are inclined to ask, "How would you behave differently if you had high self-esteem?" or "How would your life be different if you had high self esteem?" or "How would your significant others know that you had high self-esteem?" Making goals concrete forces the patient to identify specific steps that must be taken and sets the goal posts in a mutually agreed position, thus eliminating goals that cannot be observed or specified. The risk is that patients with a vague, global goal will never be able to adequately assess if they have met their treatment goals and expectations. This can lead to various kinds of discounting or minimizing actual progress in treatment. Even more problematic, the therapist will not be able to evaluate meaningfully the progress in treatment if there are no clear benchmarks set at the beginning.

In groups, treatment goals can be developed as a part of a group process, which greatly increases the sense of group cohesion and provides useful education to group members as to realistic and appropriate goals.

Target complaints enable the therapist to determine what situations are troublesome, so that personally relevant goals for change are more readily established. Once a complaint is elicited, then it is important to determine; (a) in what situations the problem occurs; (b) what the patient thinks is the cause of the problem; (c) whether this problem has occurred frequently or rarely; (d) what strategies the patient used to cope; and finally (e) how severely the patient would rate this problem on a rating scale, e.g., from 1 (least) to 10 (most severe).

It is important to note whether the complaints reflect a high priority for the patient, or else the patient may have little motivation to work on the goals that are formulated. Goals should also be realistic. If goals are too complicated or depend on the status of too many factors, then success in achieving treatment goals may be elusive. The goal must be something that the patient can achieve independently, with a specific endpoint that is well defined.

Helping patients state the goal in a positive framework sets the stage for them to understand more clearly how they can be more in control of their time and their life to make the preferred changes in their behaviors. When people are depressed, they typically perceive their needs in terms of losses or negatives. For example, "The glass is always half empty, never half full."

Developing target complaints

Clinical Example: Developing treatment goals

Clinical Vignette
Setting Treatment Goals (Second Session)

Therapist: So today one of my goals is to talk a little more about what you'd like to get out of this. Last week we talked about a few goals for you – getting some improvement in your depressed mood and energy level – and those are really important goals.

Patient: Yeah, inertia is also a bit of a problem

Therapist: Ok, let's start by having you make a sort of "problems list," and this will become our agenda for your therapy and we'll try to make sure we stay close to your goals. Of course, they can change over time too. But this will give us a way of tracking our progress. What should we start with (for your problem list)?

Patient: It would be so nice to be able to go back to school next semester and be able to make it to all my classes and actually complete the work.

Therapist: [handing patient a pad of paper] You can actually write these down as we go for your own benefit.

Therapist: So would your first goal be to return for the fall semester?

Patient: Eventually, I would like to change my major and get a degree in engineering.

Therapist: And that's a really important personal goal?

Patient: Yes, but right now I'm not up for it.

Therapist: What's interfering with achieving this goal, because that should be on our problem list?

Patient: If I could actually make it to all my classes and do all the work – I stopped going to classes I really loved and lost interest in them.

[Patient and therapist then spend some time discussing the importance of this goal in terms of personal and family values before going on to the next problem, which happened to be skipping her medication.]

In order for the patient to determine progress in achieving a goal, it is important that some criteria for measuring the progress be introduced. The scale should be simple and highly explicit, such as rating level of enjoyment or change in mood, or how many things have been accomplished over a fixed period of time, etc.

The next step is to figure out how to implement this task successfully on a day-to-day basis. What are the barriers that might get in the way of completing the task on a daily basis, such as feeling too depressed to do anything, or too many demands for her time by other important chores? Once identified, then what can the person do to offset these barriers?

Developing realistic expectations

It is helpful to the patient if some time is taken to explain precisely what they can expect in terms of change. Patients often expect that changes will occur immediately, and the goal will be achieved quickly with little difficulty. It is important to dispel this unrealistic notion, as this can help minimize the patient's tendency to think in all-or-nothing extremes. For example, for some patients if the goal is not reached quickly, then nothing has been accomplished and the treatment is viewed as "a failure". The patient should be alerted to expect that progress toward a goal rarely occurs at a steady pace, or in a continuous direction. It is important for patients to recognize and then reward themselves for each step made toward achieving the goal. When reviewing the progress toward meeting goals, remind patients that progress is often punctuated with setbacks in between, and if one were to plot the progress of change across time it would often look like an incremental saw tooth curve.

Structuring the Session: Use of Agendas and Session Checklists

Once the patient has an understanding of the model and target goals have been established, the therapist can then begin to focus more on the structure of individual sessions, which should follow a similar pattern throughout the remainder of therapy. Having a well-structured and consistent pattern for individual sessions has a number of advantages: (1) The patient develops an expectation of what will transpire in each session and what is expected of them in making each session productive. (2) Agenda-driven sessions make it easier to keep the focus on problems and tactics highly relevant to the resolution of treatment goals. (3) Finally, it is helpful in reducing a crisis-oriented treatment mentality in which the problem of the moment comes to dominate what should be a methodological, strategic, focused, and problem-oriented treatment. Particularly for patients who are in the incipient stages of a hypomanic or manic phase of the illness, structuring the session can effectively set limits on tangential, disorganized, distracted behaviors or problems with attention. For patients who are depressed, this structured treatment approach provides consistency and direction at a time when they may be feeling immobilized and helpless.

Session structure and using session checklists

The session checklist attached in the Appendix 3 is intended to help the practitioner document session content and material covered to assure that treatment progresses in a fashion consistent with the overall treatment protocol. At the end of every session, practitioners are encouraged to review items on the Session Checklist that have been covered in the session. In group sessions, material covered in each session may vary due to group dynamics or the needs of individual members.

Setting the Agenda

As early as possible during the course of therapy (usually in the second session) it is important to begin setting an agenda for each session in order to minimize the tendency toward unstructured use of time. The therapist can explain that the major advantage of structuring the session is to make the best use of available time. The agenda should be developed in collaboration with the patient. We recommend that the agenda be written out on a white board or easel paper for both individual and group therapy so that it can be referred to easily by both the therapist and the patient when necessary to keep the session on track. The first item on the agenda, almost invariably, will be to complete a check on the patient's status at the time of the session. Often patients are asked to complete some brief measure of their mood while in the waiting room, and this then becomes the focus for the initial review in the session.

Key session element: Setting the session agenda

Key session element: The "check-in"

The second item on the agenda will be a review of work completed in the home practice assignment. Practice outside sessions is critical to the success of this treatment strategy. It is important to review the patient's homework and comment on its relevance to the particular issue under consideration in therapy at the moment, as this will encourage continued compliance in completing home practice. Often patients will fail to complete home practice assignments anyway, and this needs to be dealt with. We will discuss about this problem in greater detail later.

Key session element: Reviewing homework

After review of homework, the next agenda item might be to initiate strategies that will be helpful in accomplishing a therapy goal. This could be the introduction of a specific skill that needs to be learned, or the continued practice of a skill that was introduced earlier. During early sessions, getting more history about a certain event or period in the patient's life might also be an item on the agenda. In addition to items the therapist wants to include on the agenda, the patient should always be asked what they would like to include. Once the list is completed, the items should be prioritized in terms of time allotted for discussion of each item. This is particularly important when patients consistently come to therapy with some type of crisis. During the early stages of therapy the therapist will likely be inclined to put such items first on the agenda, and often the entire session may be absorbed in trying to resolve the crisis. While this may be essential at some points, the therapist should be alerted that it is very difficult to make progress in therapy when sessions are consistently crisis oriented. Prioritizing time allotment can help control this. It is also helpful with individuals who have a crisis orientation to put their items last on the agenda so that other items can receive attention.

It is important to underscore that, in individual or group sessions, if the patient presents with suicidal ideation or plans, a severe family crisis, or high-risk change in mental status, this must take priority over any other agenda items. In some cases, individuals or groups will require additional practice on certain skill areas to master the required skills. If this occurs, certain content will need to be shifted into the next session.

Focusing on Specific Topics or Problems Included on the Agenda

Once the agenda is fixed and times for each item have been allotted, then the focus shifts to items included on the agenda. The range of topics can be quite variable. Initially, topics usually reflect a blend of skills the patient needs to learn to achieve therapy goals, combined with specific concerns and barriers that might arise during the course of skill acquisition. Throughout the session, it is a good idea to ask the patient to summarize points that have just been covered. This enables the therapist to determine fairly quickly whether the patient understands the material as presented or whether more concrete strategies need to be used to facilitate patient comprehension. Having the patient complete active summaries also helps her or him encode and remember the key points for application outside of the session.

Homework or Home Practice Assignments

Key session element: Use of homework or home practice assignments

The patient should leave therapy with some firm idea about what she or he should be doing during the week to learn or practice a task that is the focus of therapy at that particular time. These tasks might range from simple things, such as noting how often they use a certain verbal expression, (e.g., "I should") or placing small notes at strategic places in their home where they are visible and can remind them to do a certain task (e.g., take medication), thinking about a positive feature of themselves, to more complex things, such as completing unhelpful thought records, setting up an opportunity to examine the evidence for a particular belief they have about a person, or engaging in assertion skill training. Homework assignments should be developed collaboratively with the patient, and should be clearly relevant to material being covered in the therapy session. The patient must understand the rationale for the particular assignment and agree, or at least be willing to accept the possibility, that completion of the specific home practice will enable him or her to eventually achieve specific therapy goals. The assignments should involve an activity that can be accomplished fairly easily within the time span and, for the most part, can be done without having to rely solely on the occurrence of other factors or the cooperation of other individuals. Possible barriers to successful completion should be reviewed and suggestions made on how to minimize the impact of these. Attention to these points will increase compliance in doing home practice assignments.

Final Summary of the Session

Key session element: Brief summaries and summarizing the session

After homework has been assigned, several minutes should be saved for the patient to make a final summary. The therapist might say something like: "OK, it looks like you're come up with a good assignment for practice at home this week. What do you think?" ... "Now we've covered a lot of material here today, and I wonder if we could just take a few moments here to summarize the session? What do you see as some of the key points that we brought up during the session?" The therapist should praise the patient's response, and also mention any items that were omitted. The therapist might also ask how the home practice fits into the picture, i.e., how will the home practice help achieve the goal.

Feedback and Scheduling Next Appointment

Key session element: Asking for feedback

Finally, the patient should be offered the opportunity to make any additional thoughts or questions about the session. What was good about the session? How is the therapy progressing for them? What would they like to see changed, etc.? Explain to the patient that such information will be helpful in adjusting the pacing and content of future sessions. The therapist should also take the time to comment on progress, and where possible give positive feedback to the patient. Once this is completed, the time for the next appointment should be determined and a reminder card given to the patient.

4.1.5   Middle Phase of Treatment: Skill Building – Filling up the Tool Box

Given that bipolar disorder is a chronic illness with a fluctuating course through the life span, the goal of interventions should be to provide the patient with durable skills that can be maintained with a minimal amount of external treatment support. Treatment is conducted in highly structured, agenda-driven sessions with a goal of teaching the specific basic skills of monitoring, detection of prodromes, and acquisition of appropriate coping skills to improve mood stability and to minimize the occurrence of depressive or manic episodes.

The middle phase of therapy: Filling up the tool box

The Basic Skills: Monitoring Mood, Thoughts, and Behaviors

An important initial treatment task is for each patient to develop strategies that support daily mood and activity level monitoring. We believe that monitoring (initially external and then internalized) is the *sine qua non* of this therapy, without which patients are not able to identify prodromes of illness and take action before the severe cognitive and behavioral changes that are consistent with an acute episode actually occur. Patients must have at least partial awareness and acceptance of this axiom of treatment in order for therapy to be effective. Therefore, some time and effort must be expended to be sure that this is the case. Use of a road map can often be a helpful analogy to emphasize the point. A road map is of very little use in finding your way unless you can identify your own location in relation to the other points on the map. Similarly, if you hope to have impact on mood (or behavior) you must be aware of the level and kind of mood at any moment in time and its relation to other current contingent situations or thoughts.

Basic skills: Monitoring mood, thoughts and behaviors

A critical initial task in the treatment of bipolar disorder is introducing daily mood monitoring. Several monitoring tools exist and are readily available (Sachs & Cosgrove, 1998). Variations of mood monitoring charts can be found in virtually every manual that is designed for use in structured skill-building therapies. We have revised a version of the mood graph adapted from Basco and Rush (1996), which is included as Appendix 4. The scale on their mood graph has been changed to incorporate a range of normal mood, which we refer to as the "comfort zone." This adaptation emphasizes normalizing fluctuations in mood so that small mood shifts are not seen as catastrophic indications of an impending bipolar episode. It is particularly important that patients with bipolar disorder become sensitized to small mood shifts in order to identify early prodromes. Both Lam and his colleagues (Lam et al., 2001) as well as Basco and Rush (1996) emphasize the value of identifying prodromes or early warning signs of an impending episode. Another rationale for redesigning the Mood Graph is to assure that patients appreciate the fact that normal mood does not equal "0," e.g., normal mood consists of a myriad of daily shifts. If

Teaching mood monitoring

patients are frightened of mood changes they will be likely to avoid monitoring affective shifts, with the result that they will be unable to detect changes appropriately.

It is often appropiate to introduce mood monitoring in the first or second individual or group session, with the rationale that patients should become experts in tracking their own mood states. A rationale that can be given is:

> "Mood monitoring is a way of taking charge of your health. If you can begin to identify slight mood shifts, this will allow you to plan for strategies to prevent more serious mood swings. Imagine an individual on a bicycle starting to go down a slight incline and applying the brakes. Compare this to an individual who attempts to forcefully apply the brakes near the bottom of the hill. Getting an early warning sign of problems will give you important leverage in dealing with mood shifts."

Another useful technique is to always begin sessions with a check-in, where patients are asked to bring in their mood graphs for review. This provides a quick overview of how things went over the week and is positively reinforcing for patients. If patients have forgotten to do their mood graphing or have neglected to bring it to session, work in the session to reconstruct the week retrospectively. While retrospective mood recall is subject to a number of errors, this in-session activity highlights the importance of mood graphing.

Addressing various problems with mood monitoring

Specific Issues Related to Mood Monitoring

A number of common responses are frequently raised by patients that reflect concerns about monitoring. A few of these are listed here:

Clinical Vignette

Sample Responses to Mood Monitoring Concerns

Patient: I'm a rapid cycler, my moods are constantly shifting. I have so many mood shifts in one day; I cannot keep track of them.

Response: This is an important issue that many people face. Perhaps you could consider the way Wall Street reports on daily stock movements as a way of handling this problem with your mood charting. When reporting on the movements of stocks, newspapers list the "high," "low," and "close." I wonder if this would work for you.

Patient: My mood never changes – it's always the same until I end up in the hospital.

Response: A lot of people think that's the case, before they actually try to monitor their mood on a daily basis. Would you be willing to do an experiment for a week? Would you be willing to monitor your mood and pay close attention to whether there might be just small variations in your mood? Maybe you have very small mood changes that you don't notice. Why don't we set up your scale so that it has tenths of a unit between each number?

Patient: I don't just have mood changes, I have other problems too. My mood doesn't tell the whole picture. Sometimes my mood is combined with feeling irritable, anxious, or agitated. How do I monitor these feelings?

Response: Let's work together to see what type of mood charting would work best for you. It's best to individualize this so that it's more personally meaningful for you. Do you have any ideas how we might do that? [If patient doesn't respond] Perhaps we look at separately tracking the other feelings you're having such as anxiety, irritability, and agitation.

Patient: I don't think it's very useful for me to spend time monitoring my mood.

Response: Would you be willing to give it a try and see if it is helpful? Let's have you do this as an experiment to see what you can learn about your mood.

Patient: I'm too disorganized to remember to do mood charting every day.

Response: Let's find ways that you can remind yourself to complete your mood graph. Some people like to pick a specific time of day – just before dinner, after dinner or before bedtime – do you think this would help?

Patient: Sometimes my mood is really mixed – I feel depressed and manicky at the same time – how do I chart this?

Response: What you are a saying makes a lot of sense – moods aren't one dimensional. How could we capture the different dimensions of your mood?

Patient: I don't like the mood chart you use; I've got my own format.

Response: That's great! The important thing is to consistently track you mood. If your own method works better, then stick with that.

Patient: I forgot to do my mood charting.

Response: That can happen. One way to help you remember is to put your mood graph somewhere in a prominent place. Some people put it on the refrigerator door. Some put it by their bed, so that it is the last thing they see as they are getting ready for bed. Some put it on the mirror in their bathroom. Do you think his would be helpful?

Patient: I don't really know what my mood is.

Response: Let's practice having you check your mood in the session with me, and we'll try to help you understand more about what you are feeling.

Basic Skills: Developing an "Unhelpful" Thought Record

This enables patients to experience more vividly the relation between their appraisal of particular situations and their feelings and behaviors at a particular moment in time. As noted earlier in the discussion of models, individuals who are experiencing unusual changes in mood often have an unrealistic appraisal or "distorted thoughts" about themselves, the situation they are currently in, and what might happen in the future. Furthermore, there are a number of characteristic ways that individuals tend to distort incoming information, such as negative filtering, overgeneralization, mind reading, etc. Beck, Rush, Shaw, & Emery (1979) and Burns (1999) provide more detailed information on common thinking errors.

Empirical data have demonstrated that once an individual begins to focus on their automatic thoughts and critically examine whether they might actually be distortions of a particular event or set of events, she or he becomes better equipped to come up with constructive and rational thoughts that can counteract them. This "self-intervention" can have a notable effect on typical negative emotional and behavioral reactions. As patients continue to practice the skills of monitoring and evaluating their thoughts, they become more skilled in iden-

Basic skills: The "unhelpful thought record"

Characteristic ways patients make faulty appraisals

tifying cognitive distortions, and eventually become quite effective in quickly replacing distortions with rational restructuring before these distortions have a devastating impact. Learning to identify the particular type of distortion that has occurred can facilitate this process.

As is the case with mood monitoring charts, there are many different types of thought records that are being used in clinical settings. Some of the earlier ones were labeled as "Dysfunctional Thought Record" or "Automatic Thought Record." We refer to our version as an "Unhelpful Thought Record" (see Appendix 7). We prefer to use the term "unhelpful thoughts" with patients as this has less of a pathologizing connotation than thinking "errors" or "maladaptive thoughts." We put emphasis on the fact that a particular sequence

Strategies to help patients correct thinking errors

Table 20:
Helpful Hints for Correcting Thinking Errors

- Take action:
  - Once unhelpful thoughts are identified, a survey among friends and other respected individuals in the patient's social network can enable them to see if their thoughts are appropriate.
  - Becoming a "scientist" and doing little experiments to check out predictions based on unhelpful thoughts usually has a substantive corrective influence on thinking errors.
  - Examine existing evidence to see if the thought is correct. A person who receives a poor grade on a test may think, "I always mess up on tests." They can usually contest such an answer, "I don't always do poorly. I do well in some tests."

- Watch the language:
  - Often patients use very harsh language when they talk to themselves about their progress or their specific actions. Encouraging them to talk to themselves as if they were talking to a friend or business associate can sometimes soften their negative self-appraisal.
  - Negative labels of oneself almost invariably involve a serious evaluative distortion, and can be highly depressogenic if not challenged. "I'm a loser" or "I'm an idiot" does little to help one assume a positive attitude or neutral attitude. Challenging patients to define these labels more carefully and then determine if they apply to themselves typically results in a more realistic appraisal of their worth.
  - Simply reminding patients to use more positive statements encourages language reframes. Once negative statements commonly made by the patient are identified, get him or her to write these on a 3 × 5 card, and then write a counteractive positive statement on the other side so that the dyad can be contrasted. Posting positive statements about self in visible locations around the house and workplace serves a similar purpose

Using an "advantages-disadvantages" analysis

- The scale technique – decisional balancing:
  - When patients are stuck in a particular way of thinking or doing things, have them list the advantages and disadvantages, or costs and benefits, of holding on to an idea or a behavior that is not helping them. Often this strategy can get them "off center" so that change can begin to occur. This strategy is often used in motivational interviewing. Making the technique very concrete by completing a tabular listing can often add leverage to its impact.

of thoughts in reaction to an event may be unhelpful in maintaining mood stability, rather than labeling these unhelpful thoughts as distorted or incorrect appraisals. Once individuals have learned to identify unhelpful thoughts, it is useful to identify specific types of unhelpful thoughts. Unhelpful thoughts also known as "thinking errors" are characteristic ways in which individuals tend to make incorrect appraisals.

It is a good practice to review these unhelpful thoughts in session and then give the patient a list to study at home so he or she they can quickly identify typical distortions in thinking about events that are associated with negative emotional states.

As patients become more skilled in identifying and classifying unhelpful thought patterns, they become more effective in quickly developing countering thoughts. Burns (1999) has developed a list of strategies, commonly referred to as "Ten Ways to Untwist your Thinking," to help the patient in challenging unhelpful thoughts.

Learning how to complete a thought record takes some time, and most patients need some assistance in accomplishing this task. However, with help most patients can learn to do these thought records, and eventually with continued practice they learn to do this task automatically in a situation as they are having an emotional reaction, without the need to use a form. Usually, the therapist has to go through several of these in sessions before the patient feels comfortable doing it on his or her own. The thought record can be used in group as well as individual therapy. In the clinical vignette below, we illustrate how the "unhelpful" thought record can be used in a group treatment setting. Group-based treatment offers several potential advantages in terms of cost effectiveness and the ability to impact several group members during a single intervention by relying on the group process.

Basic Skills: Summing up the Thought Record

The first step is that patients must accept that their beliefs are not immutable, objectively valid, or permanent and can be changed. Encourage patients to get into the habit of completing thought records frequently and use them liberally in therapy situations. Eventually, patients learn to do them without using the forms, and rational reconstructions occur almost as automatically as the precipitating thinking errors. Here is a list of the steps in completing a typical thought record:

Summary of the unhelpful thought record

1. Identify the distressing event.
2. Identify the automatic thoughts.
3. Rate (from 0% to 100%) the strength of each belief.
4. Identify the emotions.
5. Rate (from 0% to 100%) the strength of each emotion.
6. Categorize the thinking errors.
7. Use the helpful hints to challenge the unhelpful thinking errors.
8. Develop more adaptive reconstructions and rate the how strongly they are believed.
9. Re-rate the emotions experienced earlier and list any new emotions.
10. Determine whether change occurred in the intensity of the emotions.

Steps in developing the unhelpful thought record

Clinical dialogue:
Using the unhelpful
thought record in
a group treatment
setting

Clinical Vignette

Learning To Use the Thought Record in a Group Treatment Setting

Therapist:	This would be a good time to see how the thought record works. Does anyone recall a situation where they became upset that they would be willing to share?

Frieda, a 35-year-old single female who lives with her parents, agreed to share an upsetting event with the group. The therapist used an easel to write down Frieda's comments so that the whole group could observe how the thought record can be used.

Frieda:	Ok, this is one where I didn't lash out, but I got so depressed.
Therapist:	What was the event? Let's write that down here. Why don't you write them down, too, Frieda in your blank thought record?
Frieda:	Ok. Well I made a new friend and I expected that she'd call me and she did not call.
Therapist:	Ok. [Therapist writes verbatim what the patient says]
Frieda:	So then my thoughts were that she doesn't like me.
Therapist:	Ok, "She doesn't like me."
Frieda:	And I'm too old and boring.
Therapist:	"I'm too old and boring." Thank you for sharing this with us.
Frieda:	She's mad at me.
Therapist:	Ok. Any other thoughts?
Frieda:	She doesn't want to hang out with me.
Therapist:	Ok.
Frieda:	I'm too fat. I'm a depressing person. And I still live at home with my mom and dad.
Therapist:	Ok. [Still writing]
Frieda:	[spontaneously] Boy, I get strange thoughts.
Therapist:	What was it like writing down these thoughts?
Frieda:	Oh, it was weird, because I don't know where these thoughts come from. It doesn't even make sense. It doesn't have anything to do with the event.
Therapist:	That's a wonderful example. You've just said something important, which is these are kind of automatic thoughts that come into your mind without any prompting, and you may not even be aware of them and they may have little to do with the event.
Group Member:	But to us it does.
Therapist:	Ok, it feels like it does. So then if we looked at your feelings [goes to next column]: now, if you look you had a series of thoughts, and I wonder if there were some that were particularly painful or upsetting.
Frieda:	I started to hurt.
Therapist:	Was there a particular thought that was connected with the hurt?
Frieda:	Well, that's got me. Well, the worst was that I was still living at home.
Therapist:	Ok, what was the feeling that you had?
Frieda:	Oh, that I was incompetent.
Therapist:	Well, that's kind of a thought. Let's put that over here in the thought column. What feeling did you have?
Frieda:	Shame.
Therapist:	Ok, so you had a whole series of thoughts. Let's talk more about how those affected your mood.

Frieda:	It made me more depressed.
Therapist:	Any particular thoughts that made you depressed?
Frieda:	Well the main one is that I'm still living at home.
Therapist:	Sounds like this was an interesting experience for you to look at these thoughts after writing them down. Sounds like you felt it wasn't clear how this event caused all of these thoughts.
Frieda:	Yeah, and the funny thing was that the reason she didn't call was that she was depressed herself.
Therapist:	How did you find out? Did you try to reach her?
Frieda:	Yeah, I wrote to her and asked, "Are you mad at me?"
Therapist:	So can we look at some of the thoughts that Frieda had here and see if we can find any thinking errors?
Group Member:	To me shame is the basic thing. You're not valuable.
Therapist:	Let's look at our list of thinking errors. What would that be if we looked at our list?
Group Member:	One thing is that there is a lot generalizing about yourself from one event and it's not based on a lot of evidence.
Therapist:	Let's start with the first, "She doesn't like me". Is there a thinking error there?
Frieda:	Well, one thing is, I can't tell what people think.
Group Member:	That's right. When I go out and I see people looking at me and I begin to imagine all sorts of things they are thinking. But I really can't tell what they're thinking and I forget that.
Therapist:	That's right. Then let's look at the next thought, "I'm old and boring". Is there a thinking error? How that would that fit?
Group Member:	Kind of labeling.
Therapist:	Yeah, what else?
Group Member:	Making an assumption, right? Jumping to a conclusion.
Therapist:	What about taking it personally. How would you apply that?
Group Member:	As you go through the day people look at you and you wonder what they're thinking and you don't know, so we read our own concerns into it.
Frieda:	Right!

Basic Skills: Behavioral Strategies – the Power of Pleasant Events

The work of Lewinsohn and his colleagues (Lewinsohn et al., 1986) has clearly demonstrated the relationship between depression and daily life events. When individuals experience life events that decrease their level of pleasure, mood tends to go down. Conversely, as the number of pleasurable events increases for individuals, their mood typically improves. The reciprocal relationship between level of pleasurable events and mood level is quite evident. For example, when an event occurs that results in decreased pleasant events, then mood is lowered. When mood is lowered, then individuals tend to become less active. This in turn decreases the likelihood that the individual will engage in activities that will bring pleasure into their lives, and the level of pleasant events becomes even lower. A person gets depressed so they withdraw and become socially isolated, which may negatively affect their job performance, decrease positive social interactions, etc., which makes the depression worse, which in turn decreases activity even further, and so the vicious downward spiral goes on, leading to a clinical mood disorder and all the relevant sequelae.

Basic skills:
Behavioral strategies

It is noteworthy that the reverse effect also holds. Thus, if therapists can get depressed patients to increase their level of pleasant activities on a daily basis, then their mood is improved and their symptoms of depression are reduced. If this problem is approached systematically, patients can and do develop the skills required to increase and sustain pleasurable activities at a level that tends to offset negative life events, and this in turn can prevent or decrease the frequency and severity of subsequent depressive episodes.

Several skills are needed to accomplish this. First, patients must learn to monitor mood, which we discussed earlier. As they begin to do this on a routine basis, they are encouraged to look for events of the day that may be making their mood go up or down. With the therapist's help it does not take long for the patient to see the connection between events and mood.

This realization becomes the rationale for the next step, and that is to determine what kinds of events or activities are pleasurable and what kinds are not. Through collaborative effort the patient and therapist come up with an individualized short list of pleasant activities that are practical to do on a daily basis, but are not being done by the patient at the present time. These activities could include such things as having coffee with a friend, reading a good book, visiting the local museum, walking and sitting by a nearby creek, etc. It is a good idea to try to come up with 20 or so activities and then ask the client to narrow this down to roughly 10 or so that they would be willing to try to do as often as possible during the next week. Once this list is complete, the patient is encouraged to engage in as many as possible and record how many she or he does each day. The patient should also be asked to continue daily mood monitoring, and bring both of these records to the next therapy session. Figure 2 illustrates a form that could be used for tracking pleasant events.

Tracking pleasant events

Pleasant Events	Days						
	1	2	3	4	5	6	7
1. Reading							
2. Hiking in rancho park							
3. Lunch with a friend							
4. NY Times puzzle							
5. Guided nature hikes							
6. Cooking							
7. Practicing the piano							
8. Reading the newspaper							
9. Computer browsing							
10. Listening to music							
Totals							

Figure 2
Tracking pleasant events

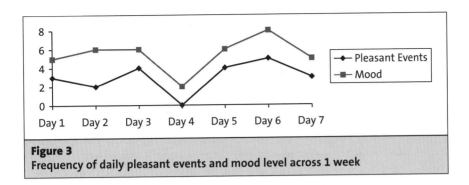

Figure 3
Frequency of daily pleasant events and mood level across 1 week

The therapist can make a graph showing the coincident changes between activities and mood level which can become a focus of discussion in the session. Figure 3 shows such a graph for a patient. Patients quickly experience an "Aha!" insight, recognizing the power of pleasure at work in their own lives. The "take-home message" for the patient is: (a) Certain kinds of events control mood; (b) You can control many of these events: (c) Therefore, you can control mood. Once this message is fully appreciated the groundwork is in place for continued problem solving to increase pleasant events on a daily basis.

Basic Skills: Identifying Early Warning Signs

Another critical skill is learning to identify early warning signs or prodromes of an impending episode. This skill can be particularly helpful when attempting to interrupt an impending manic episode (Lam et al., 1999). As noted earlier, the rationale for this is that it is much easier to make successful self-interventions to prevent an episode before it gets underway than it is to reverse the episode once it is in full force. Recognition of early warning signs appears to be difficult for bipolar patients, particularly if they are slipping into a manic episode. For depressive episodes, patients often report a feeling of being on a "slippery slope" – that they descend by slight degrees to the bottom without realizing how depressed they actually feel along the way until they have "hit bottom." Often the signs are more clearly evident to others, such as family members or professionals and nonprofessionals who interact with them on a near daily basis, long before the patient is aware of the seriousness of the problem. And then it is frequently too late to reverse the process without considerable effort on the part of the patient, as well as the relevant mental health professionals who are involved in the patient's treatment program.

Concentrated effort and repeated review of early warning sign cues is typically needed before patients are able to identify early warning signs reliably. The process is best started by first having patients identify symptoms they have when they are in a manic episode and when they are depressed. A symptom checklist, such as those in the Appendixes 5 and 6, can help patients recall symptoms in four domains, affective, behavioral, cognitive, and somatic/physiological. Each patient will have an individualized list, though many may report similar symptom patterns. Completion of this exercise will enable patients to see the similarities and differences in the symptom patterns associated with manic and depressive episodes. This is important because the treatment protocol will vary depending upon the type of episode they are experiencing. It also enables

Basic skills: Identifying early warning signs

the patient to view the total spectrum of behaviors that might be implicated in an episode. The patient learns to look for more than just mood shifts to judge whether an episode is imminent. For example, one high-level executive was alerted that a possible episode might be forthcoming when there were only a few times remaining in her appointment book to schedule new appointments. Another man programmed his computer to alert him that an episode might be starting when he spent too much time in chat rooms and contacting friends by e-mail to discuss complicated breakthroughs that revealed his "true personality." A third, who had a near uncontrollable penchant for unique and expensive foreign cars, learned that he should call his psychiatrist or his case worker immediately when he began to scan foreign car ads in the newspaper.

Once patients have a good awareness of the kinds of symptoms that might occur in each of the four domains listed above, then the focus can turn to what might be the earliest signs and symptoms. We use a symptom checklist form adapted from Basco and Rush (1996) that asks the patient to try to categorize the symptoms in each domain into those that appear early in the course of an episode, those that occur as the episode is clearly developing, and those that are readily apparent when an episode is at or near its most severe stage. Learning how to break the progression of symptoms down in this manner sets the stage for greater attention to very early prodromal moods or behaviors that are indicative of possible things to come. This process is particularly well-suited for group treatment, because disclosure by some can provide useful tips to help other members identify early ominous features in their own behavior. The clinical vignette below is an example taken from a group treatment session.

Clinical dialogue: Identifying early warning signs in a group treatment setting

Clinical Vignette
Clinical Vignette: Identifying Early Warning Signs

Therapist: Can we go back now to the symptom checklist? Did others have any problems listing symptoms they have when they're depressed and when they're manic?

Group Members agreed that they had little difficulty thinking of some symptoms, and during the conversation many were able to add symptoms that they had forgot to include.

Therapist: Ok, now we want to start thinking about what are the earliest possible indicators that you're getting depressed or starting into a manic stage.

Group Member: I have depression all the time it seems.

Therapist: Ok, let's start by finding out what makes depression worse. What are things that make your depression worse? [Therapist writes items on the white board.] If any of these apply to you and you don't have them on your list, then it's a good idea to write them down.

Group Member: Not enough sleep.

Group members continue to list different factors, including: Isolation, weight gain, lack of support, irritating advice, not taking medication on schedule, hearing or seeing something that sets off a chain of negative thoughts.

Therapist: Ok. Now let's list some of the things that make mania worse.

Group Member: Not enough sleep. [Group laughs.]

Group continues to list items while therapist writes them on the white board. List included: Ruminating on stressful situations, Sense of urgency, Uncontrollable sense of pressure, Having trouble prioritizing things, Having people tell me what I can and can't do, Not taking medication on schedule, Having weird thoughts, Trying to get things done and people or something gets in the way, Getting irritable.

Therapist: Ok. These are pretty good lists of things that make depression and mania worse. We want to keep working on the idea of finding out what are the earliest possible signs that we're sliding into a deeper depression or into a manic state. Paying attention to these things on the list may help us begin to spot changes in ourselves earlier than we have before. For our home practice this week does anyone have a good idea about how we can do this?

Group Member: Well one thing is if we keep trying to add things to our lists, maybe we can spot more things that get to us early on, and we can notice how that's affecting us.

Group Member: Also if we think about the level of these different things. Maybe some start off real gradual and we don't notice it. Maybe if we tried to see if that's the case. Like what am I doing or experiencing before I notice that I'm starting to have sleep problems.

Therapist: Well those are good suggestions. Any others?

Group Member: Maybe there are things that occur before the things that we notice. I think it would be helpful to look for things like that.

Therapist: Ok then. Our assignment for next week will be to continue looking for items to put on our list, and keep thinking about what might be happening even before or just as our mood is starting to change significantly. Going back to our symptom list, the features we've listed here are pretty obvious and we have little difficulty in identifying them. However, in many of us there may be early subtle signs that we and others don't see right away. So what we want to do is to see if we identify signs that occur very early, even before we see these more obvious symptoms. We can use the handout I gave you to list what we think are early, middle, and late symptoms for us and bring this in next week. Oh, and also we want to keep monitoring our mood. So for next week we'll have our mood graphs to hand in, and we'll have our list of early middle and late signs started so that we can finish it during our session.

A standardized list of prodromes may miss key idiosyncratic prodromes for the patient, and furthermore patients may endorse items indiscriminately. Using an open-ended interview process assures that patients will identify personally meaningful prodromes. Patients should be prompted to identify prodromes associated with each of the following domains: mood, behavioral, cognitive, and somatic changes. A form for listing individual characteristics in these four categories that are likely to occur when the patient is depressed or manic is included in Appendix 5. Once these have been identified then it is useful to determine whether each characteristic occurs in the early stages of the episode or later on (Basco & Rush, 1996; Lam et al., 1999). A companion form for this exercise is also included in Appendix 6. Then, as characteristics are identified in terms of when they occur in the course of an episode, the therapist and patient can work together to break these down even further to look for more subtle changes that might be the precursors to these identifiable characteristics.

Using idiosyncratic lists of prodromes

At this level of analysis it is important to look for cross-categorical precursors. For example, a particular behavioral trait might reappear, like foot tapping or knuckle cracking or that every appointment must be recorded in a certain way, and these may tend to be overlooked as being of any significance. However, at some very low level of awareness, this behavioral change may be serving to alert one to suspect that something may be out of kilter, and this appraisal in turn heightens the level of tension and anxiety, which then reciprocally increases the likelihood of behavioral tension and more distorted thinking, etc.

Typically, most patients can readily recognize late-stage signs of illness which may include hospitalization, psychosis, severe disorganization, or severe lethargy and psychomotor retardation. Patients will need some prompting to recall earlier signs. Early signs of depression, which often have an insidious onset, may be particularly challenging. Early signs of mania are more readily identified, with the proviso that patients may mistake early signs as evidence of apparent recovery from a depressed episode. For example, one patient identified "My thinking becomes clearer" as a prodrome of mania.

Anchoring prodromes in a social context

Ideally, prodromes will be anchored or imbedded in a social context. Frequently, family members, a significant other, or coworkers can detect such small changes some time before the patient becomes aware that they are happening, and under the right circumstances they can communicate their observations to the patient. However, there are other effective procedures that the patient can do to help identify very early signs and symptoms. It is often helpful to ask patients to begin monitoring their mood prior to this procedure and to develop some form of Life Chart which traces the progression of several key past episodes. Inquiry about how they were thinking, feeling, and behaving during various stages of past episodes will help personalize the procedure and make it concrete and specific. A brief explanation of the concept of stages of mania and depression prepares the patient for inquiries about signs of severe mania and depression and sets the stage for repetitive exploration with the therapist to identify the characteristic changes that occur during the middle stages and, finally, the earliest signs of an incipient episode. In group therapy, this can be a group exercise in which individual group members help complete an "Early-middle-late stage diagram" on the whiteboard or easel pad. This is especially helpful in consolidating group cohesion and giving group members a chance to educate each other.

Basic Skills: Developing Coping Plans

Basic skills: Developing coping plans

As is the case in all other facets of this therapy, collaborative work with patients is a key to success in identifying useful coping strategies that are personally meaningful and likely to be used in an effective and timely manner. A key goal in many effective treatment approaches for bipolar disorder is to help the patients develop specific, realistic, and concrete coping plans that will enable them take constructive action when they next experience the beginning of an episode of mania or depression. In order to be effective, coping plans must be individually tailored to each patient and must reflect specific strategies that have high feasibility and are likely to occur. Lam et al. (1999) suggest that coping strategies be individualized because of the unique "relapse signature" for each patient. The underlying philosophy around development of coping strategies is a belief that patients can and must take an active, participatory role in treatment if they are to receive the full benefits of therapy. In order to actively manage their bipolar illness, patients will need to learn about their illness and develop a collaborative relationship with their healthcare professionals including: (1) becoming an expert in medication and actively participating in decisions about medication; and (2) monitoring and regulating their mood by identifying key cognitions and behaviors.

Developing coping strategies can be initiated simply by inquiring about what has been most helpful in the past and making a list of potential strategies. The therapist and patient will then carefully review the list and prioritize the best strategies in terms of feasibility and likelihood of achieving success. There are useful psychoeducational materials that we routinely recommend to patients that can provide a general discussion of the rational for coping strategies; however, these materials cannot substitute for an individualized approach. Some therapists have experimented with using a list of standard coping strategies; again, we find it preferable to "discover" strategies with the patient. This discovery process, and ultimately testing out solutions in action, is an extremely powerful tool in helping the patient believe in the value of these coping skills.

Basic Skills: Addressing Manic and Hypomanic Thinking and Behaviors in the Session

Patients in the hypomania and mania phases of bipolar disorder present a significant therapeutic challenge. Clinicians are quite familiar with addressing negative emotions such as anxiety and depression that appear as key symptoms across all the major psychiatric disorders, but the hypomanic-manic state involving an extreme sense of well-being, euphoria, a high level of energy and productivity, and high levels of optimism appears to be quite unique as a psychiatric condition. Hypomania in its milder forma can be associated with increases in creativity and productivity and a number of other positive effects. Clinicians have long recognized that the pure euphoria of mania is seductive and that patients often appear to engage in a number of behaviors that suggest that they are "addicted to mania."

Basic skills: Addressing manic and hypomanic thinking and behaviors

This romantic view of mania fails to address the patient's experience of dysphoric mania and mixed states in which symptoms of depression, anxiety, and mania may coexist. In our experience, these mixed states with significant anxiety, unpleasant overactivation, and disorganized thinking are all too common, although patients will tend to be selective in their recall of the positive effects of mania. Unfortunately, hypomania and manic states also include loss of judgment and engaging in high-risk pleasure-seeking behaviors that ultimately have very painful emotional, financial, and interpersonal consequences.

Debunking the romance of mania

For the hypomanic patient, the combination of poor judgment and underestimating the risk and negative consequences of impulsive actions, combined with a heightened level of activation, often results in very negative consequences. The damage done during even a brief manic episode in terms of burning bridges and causing financial and interpersonal damage can be absolutely disastrous.

Interviewing Style With Patients Who Are Manic or Hypomanic

You may need to adjust your interviewing style with patients who present with hypomanic or manic phase presentations. In general, consider that patients in these states are likely to be irritable, easily angered, distracted, and overactive

Interview styles with patients who are manic or hypomanic

Table 21
Interview Style with the Hypomanic/Manic Patient

Do's	Don't's
Sit quietly	Sit too close
Avoid any rapid movements	Sit away from the door
Keep personal space	Argue or debate
Use Socratic questioning	Challenge or confront the patient
Use a calm tone of voice	Blame or shame
Speak slowly	Lecture
Use open-ended questions	Tell the patient what to do
Engage patient in a collaborative fashion	Be "the expert" on mania
Encourage "sitting and talking"	

(talking too much, over-talking, not listening, etc.). It is important to "slow it down" in the session and avoid overstimulating the patient. Table 21 provides some suggestions that can be helpful when attempting to work with patients in a state of mania. It is important to use respectful caution when dealing with individuals who are at the apex of a manic episode. Attempts to impose constraints of any sort can often lead to violent outbursts, for which the parties responsible later are often exceedingly remorseful.

Helping Patients Assess Hypomanic States

Basic skills: Helping patients assess hypomanic states collaboratively

A powerful tool for helping patients assess the current risk for hypomania is the use of a "Weighing the Evidence" intervention. One of the clinical issues in addressing possible hypomania and the need to take steps to prevent full-blown mania is that hypomanic patients can be irritable, especially if they feel confronted or challenged. It is extremely important that the therapist take a highly collaborative approach with patients in this irritable, hypomania state. At the same time, this represents a perfect opportunity to help the patient identify risks for mania and to develop strategies to control hypomania. Ideally, the therapist will have developed a list of warning signs with the patient when the patient was in a euthymic state. This list can now be reviewed collaboratively to assess for the risk of hypomania.

Clinical vignette: Helping patients assess the risk of hypomania

Clinical Vignette
Helping Patients Assess Risk of Hypomania

A 32-year-old Asian-American woman comes to group session 4 of a specialty bipolar disorder treatment group, indicating that she had only 3 hours of sleep last night. She denies that she is at risk of becoming manic, despite feedback from other group members, and in fact insists that this sleep loss is helpful in combating depression. However, she does agree to participate in an exercise reviewing the evidence that she might be becoming manic.

Therapist: So you're telling me that there was such a pressure to do things that you couldn't sleep? Is that right? Did I mishear you?
Patient: Yeah, that's right.

Therapist:	But you're saying you're not worried about becoming manic or hypomanic?
Other Patient:	When I lose that much sleep I become irritable and hypomanic, but I feel like I can write a whole book.
Patient:	Yeah, you discover all these talents. By pulling an "all nighter" last week, I changed my body chemistry.
Therapist:	This seems really important. Could we look at the evidence that this is just a normal mood range for you or something more?
Patient:	Well, I'm a bit irritable. [Evidence of hypomania]
Therapist:	Ok, [going to board and writing] could we look at the evidence for "I'm not hypomanic" versus the evidence for "I am hypomanic." Are you willing to work with me here?
Patient:	OK.
Therapist:	Let's look at the evidence that you're really OK – you're not getting into trouble-hypomania.
Patient:	I'm a little irritable.
Therapist:	That's probably on the side of hypomania. Right?
Patient:	But, I'm not going on shopping sprees.
Therapist:	Let's look at all the evidence that you're OK. What else?
Patient:	Well, I did go on a shopping spree, but I returned half the stuff.
Therapist:	I'm a little confused. Maybe we should put the shopping spree on one side [Manic] and the returns on the other (not manic)? [Laughter from group members]
Patient:	I also feel more positive and optimistic. I realize now the obsessive thoughts I had (when depressed) were unfounded.
Therapist:	So all these are pretty much evidence that you're feeling better, right? Are these all reflections of your normal mood state? Is this how you usually feel – optimistic and positive all the time? So these are signs of normal mood for you?
Patient:	Well, my speech is a bit rapid.
Therapist:	So, where is the evidence that you might be getting hypomanic?
Patient:	Irritability is a sign, right?
Therapist:	And, I guess, shopping sprees, although you returned half the stuff and that's on the "evidence against" side.
Patient:	I'm feeling more social too.
Therapist:	What else should be on the list? What about you're sleeping 4 hours a night?
Patient:	Yes.
Therapist:	So is this a balanced picture? How do you weigh the evidence at this point?
Patient:	Is there anything between normal and hypomania?
Therapist:	Sure. Let's put the question this way: Are you 100% sure that you are in a normal mood state and there's no possibility that you're getting hypomanic?
Patient:	I'm 100% convinced I'm somewhere between normal and hypomanic.
Therapist:	Ok, what do you need to do now? If you're not 100% convinced, that's a sign that you may need to consider taking some action now.

Developing Coping Strategies to Target Hypomania

In our experience, behavioral strategies have proven to be more effective in addressing hypomanic and manic behaviors. These strategies aim to delay impulsive behaviors with a high likelihood of negative consequences and challenge hyperpositive, grandiose thinking associated with mania and hypomania.

Developing coping strategies to target hypomania

The hypomania
toolbox: Behavioral
strategies

Table 22
Behavioral Strategies "Toolbox" to Combat Hypomania

- Increase monitoring of hypomanic symptoms
- Encourage patient to call doctor and get a PRN
- Avoid activating situations – help patient plan to avoid provocative situations or people
- Instruct patient and family members to "disengage"
- Make a list assigning priorities to tasks (Basco & Rush, 1996)
- Brainstorm three ways to relax
- Address sleep disruption
- Reframe hypomania as stress and have patient review "coping with stress list"
- Assign calming and soothing activities
- Invoke the 48-hour rule (Newman et al., 2002)
- Ask two friends first.
- "More sitting and listening"(Newman et al., 2002)
- Reviewing the evidence – use Socratic questioning to review signs of mania
- Review patient's "Signs of Mania Worksheet" (previously completed in euthymic state)
- Use a role reversal and have patient argue against the impulse
- Develop a specific advantages/disadvantages list to review the impulsive behavior
- Review possible negative outcomes – brainstorming collaboratively with the patient
- Suggest an "empirical test" to encourage patient to monitor their signs of mania/hypomania
- Review previously developed "Coping Plan"
- Help patient challenge overly positive predictions ("It's all going turn out great" – predicting the future) and emotional reasoning ("I know I am going to win the lottery because I feel so lucky today, I can't lose")

The hypomania
toolbox: Cognitive
strategies

However, often cognitive and behavioral strategies are used in combination. Table 22 lists a number of therapeutic strategies for helping patients that have been culled from several sources, including Basco and Rush (1996), Lam et al. (1999), Newman et al. (2002), and Miklowitz (2002).

If the patient is willing, then "The devil's advocate role play technique" (Newman et al., 2002) can be quite helpful. In this procedure the therapist plays the role of the patient and the patient as therapist explores with you the risks of hypomanic behavior. When done in a group setting it is not uncommon for other group members to contribute ideas to the patient (as therapist) to try out on the therapist (as patient), and this sometimes can solidify a balance sheet of advantages and disadvantage if one continues to engage in hypomanic behaviors. "The 48-hour rule" (Newman et al., 2002) is a strategy where the therapist or group suggests that if it's a great idea right now then it will still be a good idea in 48 hours. "So, would it be a good idea to wait and see?" The goal is to help the patient slow down and avoid reckless, impulsive decision-making. "Ask two friends first" is a technique where the patient agrees that before they go out and act on their idea they will ask two trusted friends first concerning their opinion. Again, the goal of this intervention is to get the patient to slow down and get feedback before engaging in overly impulsive goal-driven behaviors. "More sitting and listening" (Newman et al., 2002)

Clinical Vignette

Intervening in Hypomania, "I'm Feeling Really Good – I Can't Lose"

Mr. M found he had extra energy at work over the past week and began staying late to catch up on projects. He was enjoying his increased confidence and energy and felt very productive. However, he began to notice that he was having more trouble getting to sleep at night, sometimes taking two to three hours to "settle down." On the way home on the next night, he decided to stop at the local bar and have a few drinks in order to calm down. He immediately noticed a very attractive woman at the bar and struck up a discussion with her. He felt particularly witty and charming.

The next day, he also noticed that he was a little shorter than usual with his co-workers. The following night he was quite irritable with his wife and felt annoyed with her that she could not "keep up" with him in their conversation and seemed not to understand what he was saying. It seemed to him that his mind was working more clearly now and he wondered if he still needed to take his lithium since he felt "well." In fact, he had a number of exciting ideas he wanted to discuss with his boss that he was sure would get him noticed and probably promoted. "It was a sure thing", he thought to himself and felt really good about his prospects.

Table 23
Identifying Thinking Errors in Hypomania

Predicted Positive Outcomes	Possible Thinking Errors
"I know I'll really impress my boss."	Predicting the positive
"I can't lose."	Underestimating risk
"This is a sure fire thing. I'll get promoted."	Misreading the reactions of others

emphasizes the need to exert control overactivity, impulsiveness, and an action-oriented schema by paying more attention to feedback and the importance of the interpersonal and social context.

Any number of the strategies listed in Table 23 might be helpful with Mr. M. If he is familiar with the "Unhelpful Thought Record" and its use in cognitive restructuring, then a variation of this approach highlighted in Tables 23 and 24 can also be useful. The first step is for the patient to see if there are possible thinking errors in his ideas. The therapist can work collaboratively with Socratic questioning to see if any thinking errors can be identified by Mr. M. It is noteworthy that patients may not identify thinking errors at the moment, and they might emphatically reject any that are suggested. However, when asked to reflect later on the evidence for and against the presence of thinking errors, they may often apply the information brought forth in the session while re-examining their ideas.

Once the patient is aware of possible thinking errors, it is possible then to develop constructive challenges. Table 24 provides some challenges to a patient's hypomanic thinking.

Challenging hypomanic thinking

Table 24
Challenging hypomanic thinking

Predicted Positive Outcomes	Challenges
"I know I'll really impress my boss."	If it's a really great idea, then it's ok to wait 24 hours before proceeding.
"I can't lose."	Have you discussed this with other coworkers and gotten feedback?
"This is a sure fire thing. I'll get promoted"	Is it *at all possible* that your boss may not agree with your idea? Are there any warning signs that you might be getting high?

Summing It All Up

The following case illustrates how monitoring of mood changes, identifying prodromes, and developing a coping plan can be prophylactic even against severe episodes of illness.

Clinical vignette: Developing coping strategies for a psychotic episode

Clinical Vignette

The Case of Bill – Developing Coping Strategies for a Psychotic Episode

Bill is a 40-year-old Caucasian male. He lives with his girlfriend of 18 years. His girlfriend provides financial and emotional support for him. He has had a sporadic work history, is not currently working, and has held five jobs in the last 5 years with an average length of 6 months at each job. His presenting problems and current concerns focused on feeling anxious and overwhelmed. He presented as motivated for treatment, pleasant, articulate, bright, and relatively able to be insightful except during manic episodes. His partner was supportive of therapy and involved in coping plans developed by patient. Bill's treatment goals are identified in Table 25.

Bill was first diagnosed in 1981, at age 17, with bipolar disorder, which he attributed to "high school stress." The most recent of three psychiatric hospitalizations in June of 2003 was for a severe manic episode with psychotic features (including delusions of grandeur). He attributed the episode to changes in medication and stress.

There was a family history of bipolar disorder on his father's side of the family. Currently, his treatment involved outpatient medication management one time per month treated with divalproex (Depakote, 2000 mg) and olanzapine (Zyprexa; recently increased to 20 mg and PRN) and outpatient group therapy once a week in a specialized treatment program for bipolar disorder.

The therapeutic work with Bill focused on identifying and monitoring early prodromal signs of mania and becoming aware of how stressful situations increased his risk of illness. Bill began regularly monitoring his mood on a daily basis using a mood monitoring graph adapted from Basco and Rush (1996) over a period of several weeks. He regularly completed his mood monitoring where he typically rated himself in the "0" to "+2" range, indicating normal or slightly elevated mood in the normal range. In addition, Bill developed a set of early warning indicators that acted as "red flags" for previous episodes and he identified specific coping strategies that he could use when he identified the onset of hypomania.

Clinical vignette:
Identifying warning
signs

Bill identified the following early warning signs of a hypomanic/manic episode:
- Feeling more "keyed up" and having trouble settling down
- Feeling stressed
- Starting to lose sleep
- Beginning to experience unusual thoughts and feelings
- Becoming secretive and hiding these thoughts and feelings from his partner

Bill developed the following coping plan for hypomania/ mania:
- Deep breathing and meditation
- Talk to significant other
- Call doctor
- Make medication changes
- Prioritize activities
- Slow down: don't drive on freeway; don't react to other drivers
- Avoid overstimulation: avoid arguments; avoid ruminating

Several weeks into the treatment program, Bill began to experience increasing signs of activation and complained about stressors he associated with selling his house and feeling pressure from girlfriend to complete tasks related to their impending move. After missing group for a week, Bill returned and reported that he had had a "mixed manic episode" this past week in which he began to experience unusual thoughts ("My desktop files are organized in a especially significant way"; "I'm part of a grand plan"; "I have a true understanding of my life") and a sense of being very buoyed up and restless. His mood graph indicated a sharp spike into the +4 to +5 range, indicating "very manic" or severe hypomania/mania.

Putting it all together

Bill was able to communicate with his girlfriend and call his doctor, with the result that he received some additional medication and did not cycle into a full manic episode that required hospitalization. This was the first such episode that Bill had been able to avoid ending up in the hospital in a severe psychotic state.

When we reviewed the different outcome for this episode, it appeared that Bill had implemented a few "small" but highly important changes, as he noted in his diary: "This time it was different, I didn't hide the episode." He was able to let his girlfriend know about the changes in his thinking instead of being secretive, and he called his doctor for the first time prior to being hospitalized. This case illustrates how careful monitoring and small, specific behavioral changes that are incorporated into a coping plan can significantly affect the outcome of a bipolar episode.

Clinical vignette:
Identifying treatment
goals

Table 25
Bill's Treatment Goals for Bipolar Disorder Group

- Openness of mood /illness with others
- Self- awareness of mood swings
- Difficulty asking for needs to be met
- Problems asserting self with others/
- Overcome fear of stigma
- Employment problems

Basic Skills: Addressing Maintenance of Social Routines and Sleep Loss

Disruption of daily routines is a major issue for most bipolar patients. It is often difficult for patients to ascertain whether some life event triggers thinking and behavioral changes that lead to sleep problems and consequent dysregulation of stable daily routines, or whether a disruption in stable daily routines leads to increased problems with sleep. Whatever the case, sleep problems are almost invariably the first symptoms mentioned by patients as an indicator

Basic skills:
Addressing
maintenance of
routines and sleep
loss

that a serious episode may be looming in the near future. The importance of attempting to rectify sleep and daily routine stability in these patients can not be overestimated. Whatever other strategies that are implemented in coping plans, these must receive heavy emphasis as well, if they are indeed seen as part of the immediate complex of behavioral changes.

Basic Skills: Developing Coping Plans for Depressive Episodes

Basic skills: Developing coping plans for depressive episodes

A number of evidence-based strategies for coping with depressive episodes have been outlined in the literature over the past 30 years. Psychological interventions with the strongest evidence based support to date for the treatment of major depressive episodes include cognitive therapy, behavioral therapy, and interpersonal therapy. In Section 4.3: Efficacy and Prognosis, we review the evidence for the effectiveness of a number of psychological treatment procedures for bipolar depression. However, it is beyond the scope of this guide to provide a detailed review of all effective approaches to the treatment of depression.

References for CBT with depression

In 1979, Beck, Rush, Shaw, and Emery (1979) developed the initial cognitive behavioral treatment manual for depression, detailing cognitive and behavioral techniques for depression. Basic strategies and techniques since that time have been consistently refined, but many of the key evidence-based strategies detailed in their excellent resource manual are still appropriate, have been tested in multiple controlled clinical trials, and are "up-to-date."

A comprehensive review of the psychological treatment of depressive episodes is beyond the scope of this book, which is intended to be a compact guide. Many of the specific techniques, such as the development of thought records, the review of cognitive errors and cognitive biases, the use of behavioral interventions such as activity scheduling, and pleasant events scheduling and the use of home practice, are also illustrated in another section (section 4.1.5). Readers who require more detailed information are referred to several easily obtained teaching and instructional resources listed at the end of the book in Chapter 5: Further Readings.

4.1.6   Final Phase: How to Maintain Treatment Gains

The final phase of treatment

The final three or four weekly sessions should be devoted to termination of therapy, how to maintain the gains made in therapy, and how to improve life management issues to minimize precipitating stressful events. Because of the chronic nature of this disorder, relapse or recurrence is more the rule rather than the exception, given the limited treatment armamentarium currently available. Thus, following the guidelines for relapse prevention developed by Marlatt and his colleagues (Marlatt, 1996), considerable emphasis is placed on strategies to minimize the occurrence of future episodes. During this period the therapist and patient review what has been learned. Discussion is focused specifically on the possibility of relapse, particularly what kinds of situations might precipitate an episode and what the patient might do in anticipation of these to minimize the probability of a full-blown episode. That is, what skills should be applied in what situations to avoid or abort an impending episode?

Ending weekly sessions can sometimes be stressful for patients, and the transition might actually precipitate an episode if the termination is too abrupt. We recommend that at the conclusion of the formal weekly therapy sessions, several booster sessions be included at biweekly intervals, in order for the patient to disengage from the therapeutic relationship, and to use independently the tools learned in therapy in order to combat or prevent severe mood swings. Booster sessions also serve as a "check-in" time to see how the patient is using her or his new skills. If possible, continued check-in sessions at monthly intervals over a period of 8–10 months can be immensely helpful to some patients in solidifying their skills and minimizing the probability of relapse or reoccurrence. During the final sessions, patients are encouraged to discuss: (1) what ending therapy means, (2) their ideas about what was more helpful and what was less helpful during treatment, and (3) their feelings about the therapist as a person. Talking directly about these issues helps create a more positive ending, and will give the patient a sense of closure that is very important. Thought records focusing on their concerns about termination can help them gain perspective on their abilities to maintain their gains.

Developing a Maintenance Guide

The "maintenance guide" is a specific, highly individualized set of guidelines created by both therapist and patient that consolidates the patient's experience in therapy, by reviewing skills and preparing for possible problems in the future. Usually, it takes about three sessions to create this document before the final summary session. It's a good idea to start this guide in session and then have the patient complete, or add to it for homework.

Relapse protection: Developing the maintenance guide

1. **Review skills learned.** Development of the guide begins by asking the patient to review the skills learned throughout therapy. The patient is told: "To begin the preparation of your maintenance guide, it's a good idea to list what specific skills you have learned in therapy that you feel are going to be useful to you in the future, for avoiding serious mood swings. Spend a few minutes now to think about all of the skills you learned, and then list them in the categories of the cognitive, behavioral, and interpersonal skills you have learned during therapy. "

Relapse protection: Reviewing skills learned in therapy

2. **Identify situations that are potentially stressful.** Ask the patient to think about and make a list of the situations that are likely to arise in the future that may exacerbate symptoms and result in mood swings. For example: "What kinds of high-risk situations might occur in the future that would trigger thoughts, emotions, or behaviors that could start an episode?" Encourage the patient to take time to think carefully about the fact that there are certain situations likely to arise in the future that will tend to disrupt their lives in some way that may precipitate an episode. Say to the patient, "Now is a good time to think about which situations or events might do this, and to make a list, so that you can see how the tools you have learned in therapy will help you handle these situations differently the next time around." List some relevant examples for them and then comment, "Any one of these events may be stressful, but they do not necessarily have to result in an episode if you're prepared. You can use the tools you have learned here to offset the stress and keep stability in your life. Now is the time to develop your own personal list of events or situations that are (a) likely to occur after therapy ends, and (b) likely to cause you to disrupt your life and slip into an episode of depression or mania. Ask yourself: 'What kinds of high

Relapse protection: Identifying potential triggers or stressful situations

risk situations might I experience that would send my thoughts, feelings and my behaviors into a whirlwind, whether up or down?'"

3. **Identify appropriate strategies for each stressful situation.** After the list is generated, ask the patient to think of specific behavioral and cognitive skills (from the earlier list) that would help in each particular situation. "Now that you have this list, try to think of which specific skills that you listed earlier would help with each particular situation." It is helpful to start this process in sessions so that the therapist and other group members, if therapy is being conducted in a group, can discuss the details and make additional notes about which of the ideas brought up by the patient might be most helpful. The patient can continue the activity as a homework assignment and additional points can be added during the next session.

4. **Recognizing early warning signs.** Encourage the patient to talk about early warning signs that might alert the individual that they are experiencing a mood shift again and this may become more severe if action is not taken. The goal is to work out a concrete plan of action, including very specifically what to do and who to call, etc. Patients should think about past episodes and try to identify what were the most significant indicators that a serious episode was underway or about to start. It is helpful for patients to make a list of actions and reactions that they would consider to be their warning signs. This can sensitize patients to be on the alert for these in the future, in sufficient time to make immediate plans for constructive action.

The topic can be introduced by the therapist reminding the patient that it is important to be prepared for future problems should they arise. Some variation of the following conversation could introduce the topic:

"Knowing your 'early warning signs' is crucial to maintaining your well-being. Future negative events are likely to occur, and you may be successful in implementing your coping plan to handle them. However, there may be times when, for some reason, the tools you have are not adequate and do not prevent a mood swing. This can happen, despite our best efforts. It is nothing to be ashamed of. The important thing for you is to know when you have reached a point where you know you're not able to handle the situation, so that you can seek professional assistance before it gets even worse. The answer, of course, is different for each person. It can be helpful now to think back to the most recent episode and try to remember what your main symptoms were. Did you mainly have trouble eating, sleeping, with your energy level, or were your thoughts racing and you felt invincible? Were you primarily sad, angry, anxious, or perhaps lonely, in terms of mood? What was your functioning like? What we're trying to do here is to clarify which symptoms are more significant in terms of signaling a serious mood swing. It's helpful to list these so-called warning signs, so that you can be more sensitive to their occurrence in the future. This will help you learn to take action right away."

Finally, such discussions about potential future problems helps normalize this phenomenon, which can minimize the stigma associated with failed attempts to adapt, and thus may lead to more rapid attempts to obtain help when needed.

5. **Know what to do when early warning signs occur.** It is important to have an established concrete plan that provides details on what to do in the event

that warning signs surface. Who can the patient call? What might be a good back-up plan in case appropriate help can not be obtained, etc.? Specific answers to such questions organized into a plan of action can be comforting to both therapist and patient as termination approaches and long-term maintenance begins. Finally, the patient should be reminded that an important resource can be found in the homework assignments and other materials collected during the course of therapy, and should be encouraged to review periodically the written notes and workbook materials.

4.2 Mechanisms of Action

This section reviews the hypothesized mechanisms of action in the following evidence-based treatment strategies:
–   Targeted psychoeducation and illness management strategies
–   Monitoring activities and mood
–   Interpersonal and social rhythm therapy
–   Family-focused treatment
–   Cognitive-behavioral treatment approaches

4.2.1 Targeted Psychoeducation and Illness Management Strategies

Psychoeducational and illness management strategies are designed to provide patients with information about the nature and causes of psychiatric disorders, give them a clear rationale for seeking and remaining in treatment (including staying on medication), and help them develop effective self-management skills, including managing stressors effectively, identifying warning signs of new episodes, developing specific coping skills, and formulating a relapse plan. The main rationale is that improving compliance with treatment, especially medication, and assisting patients in the management of potentially stressful situations can ameliorate the course of future episodes by helping the patient identify protective strategies and reduce high-risk behaviors (medication nonadherence, substance use, excessive interpersonal or family conflict, impulsive decision-making, etc.).

Mechanisms of action: Psychoeducation

4.2.2 Monitoring of Activities and Moods

Monitoring of behaviors and emotional states is the cornerstone of nearly all cognitive-behavioral therapies. As noted above, two large well-designed randomized controlled clinical trials (Colom et al., 2003; Lam et al., 2003) utilizing mood monitoring and identification of prodromes have demonstrated significant improvements in a number of outcomes related to recurrence of bipolar episodes. Monitoring provides information to the patient, which enables him or her to become aware of important contingencies embedded in the complaints. This is the first step in making decisions about why and how

Mechanisms of action: Monitoring

to initiate corrective therapeutic strategies. Both prospective and retrospective monitoring is incorporated in the life chart method (NIMH-LCM) developed by the National Institute of Mental Health (NIMH) as a key intervention in assisting the patient and therapist in monitoring the longitudinal course of bipolar disorder for both assessment and treatment purposes. Plotting the course of illness both retrospectively and prospectively serves to clarify the role of psychosocial stressors and medication adherence in the treatment of past episodes and develops a collaborative empirical approach that enhances adherence to treatment (Post et al., 1988)

There is significant empirical evidence from a variety of published clinical trials that establishes the value of mood monitoring in affective disorders and specifically establishes the effectiveness of mood monitoring for patients with bipolar disorder. For example, some form of clinical monitoring is incorporated as a key intervention in several clinical trials of patients with bipolar disorder by multiple investigators (Frank et al., 1997; Lam et al., 2003; Colom et al., 2003). Gary Sachs, MD, the principal investigator of the NIMH-funded multicenter STEP-BD program, utilizes mood graphing as one of the primary clinical tools provided on his web-site for the Harvard Mood Disorders Program (http://www.manicdepressive.org/tools.html).

Two recent large studies utilizing randomized controlled designs (Colom et al., 2003; Lam et al., 2003) demonstrate that a therapeutic focus relying on early identification of prodromes and maintenance of social rhythm stability produces significant improvements in clinical outcomes for patients with bipolar disorder versus a control group receiving standard care. The Colom study is especially interesting in that it provides a comparison to an attention-placebo control group to control for nonspecific treatment effects. The study demonstrated significant differences in recurrence rates at 2-year follow-up: 92% of subjects in the control group had a recurrence, compared to 67% in the psychoeducation group ($p<.001$). In addition, the total number of episodes was significantly lower in patients who received the experimental treatment, and a survival analysis of patients remaining in remission for each condition indicated that the control and treatment groups were significantly different in terms of time to any recurrence. The Lam study also demonstrated that a specialized cognitive-behavioral treatment including monitoring of prodromes, development of specific coping strategies, and promoting social rhythm stability was associated with significantly fewer bipolar episodes, fewer days in a bipolar episode, and fewer hospital admissions in the 12 months under study. The group receiving cognitive-behavioral treatment specifically showed less fluctuation in manic symptoms and improved coping abilities related to manic symptoms. The main therapeutic mechanism in this study appears to be helping patients monitor prodromes of illness and disruptions of social routines and rhythms and assisting them in identifying effective behavioral and cognitive coping strategies.

4.2.3   Social Rhythm Disruption as a Catalyst for Bipolar Episodes

Several researchers have theorized that the primary biological pathway to bipolar disorder is through disruptions in the individuals' circadian rhythms, and that individuals with bipolar disorder are especially sensitive to these disruptions (Frank et al., 2000; Lam et al., 1999). Malkoff-Schwartz et al. (1998) studied the degree to which social routine or rhythm disruption acts as a catalyst for manic and depressive bipolar episodes. The concept espoused is that social routines such as sleeping, eating, and periods of activity help to "entrain" circadian rhythms (Malhoff-Schwartz et al., 1998, p. 702). The investigators conclude that social routine disrupting (SRM) events over an 8-week preonset period were strongly associated with the onset of mania. For individuals with this vulnerability, instability in circadian rhythms is not self-correcting as it is in nonvulnerable populations. Disruptions can lead to increasing desynchronization or disentrainment of the sleep/wake cycle, which then leads to somatic symptoms and eventually the onset of a manic or depressive episode (Ehlers et al., 1988).

Mechanisms of action: Social rhythm disruption

4.2.4   Family-Focused Treatment

As discussed earlier, family-based treatment approaches for bipolar disorder evolved from earlier findings as to the role of negative expressed emotion (EE) in families of schizophrenics in producing higher levels of relapse and rehospitalization(Miklowitz, 2004). Family-based treatment of bipolar disorder emphasizes psychoeducation, communication skills training, and developing problem-solving skills among family members in order to reduce the level of conflict and distress in the family. Family-focused treatment recognizes the role of underlying biological/genetic vulnerability to the disorder and proposes a stress-vulnerability model that accounts for both environmental and innate biological factors. The main assumption underlying this approach is that reducing stress in the family environment can delay, minimize, or even prevent recurrences of bipolar disorder.

Mechanisms of action: Family-focused treatment

4.2.5   Cognitive-Behavioral Treatment Approaches

As indicated earlier, cognitive-behavioral therapies (CBT) have demonstrated effectiveness for major depressive episodes (Barlow, 2001; Beck et al., 1979; Lambert, 2004). The assumption is that patients are vulnerable to depressive episodes in part because of a bias in their information processing system that causes them to misconstrue or misinterpret events in a negative direction. The cognitive model posits that interventions which create changes in either thoughts or behaviors can have a reciprocal effect on feelings. Thoughts, feeling, and behavior are viewed as having a reciprocal relationship such that, for example, negative thinking ("I'm incompetent – I won't be able to do this") might lead to changes in behavior (giving up, not trying, avoiding tasks, isolating, withdrawing), which can then lead to an increasing sense of depression and even lowered self-esteem. This in turn might lead to further self-critical thoughts ("What a loser I am, I couldn't even do this simple task"), increasing immobility and a lowered mood.

Mechanisms of action: Cognitive-behavioral treatment

For patients with bipolar disorder, CBT targets distorted hypomanic thinking and high-risk behaviors in addition to depression. Hypomanic thinking is viewed as being based on distorted grandiose beliefs that underestimate the risk and liability of risk-taking and pleasure-seeking behaviors and overestimate the potential positive rewards. In the behavioral realm, hypomanic individuals are predisposed to action and have difficulty accepting delay. CBT strategies target these behaviors ("I'm going to tell the boss that he's a bastard – he's had it coming for a long time"). and associated high-risk cognitions ("It's going to work out great"). The assumption is that helping the patient challenge high-risk impulsive actions and distorted beliefs will result in an ability to counter impulsive risk-taking behavior and reduce the likelihood of serious harm. In addition, it is clear that CBT gives critical importance to the role of medication adherence and that many interventions attempt to address the patient's distorted beliefs about medication ("I'll become dependent"; "I'll lose my ability to be creative"; "I'll be hopelessly stigmatized";"Taking medication means I'm sick"). Newman et al. (2002) conclude that cognitive factors, including distortions in the patient's perceptions, information-processing, belief systems, and judgment act as primary contributors to the development of continuing episodes of illness. The treatment aims to modify the patient's beliefs, especially long-standing schema – fundamental beliefs that channel the patient's cognitive processing of events – that increase the patient's vulnerability to manic and depressed episodes. The assumption is that modification of these cognitive vulnerabilities can fortify the patient against the continuing vicious cycle of manic and depressive episodes by developing more effective coping abilities and problem solving and reducing vulnerability to stress. In addition, this treatment approach utilizes a range of behavioral interventions to assist patients in delaying impulsive actions in the manic and hypomanic phases.

4.3   Efficacy and Prognosis

This section briefly reviews efficacy and effectiveness data on psychosocial treatment, with an emphasis on surveying well-controlled trials highlighting random assignment and including a discussion of outcomes, course, and typical recurrence rates, as well as strategies to reduce relapse.

Psychosocial interventions are effective

There is substantial evidence that psychosocial interventions when added to standard medication management can improve outcomes for patients with bipolar disorder by reducing relapses and rehospitalizations, reducing both the frequency and intensity of manic and depressed episodes, increasing symptom-free survival time, and improving social skills and overall functioning and quality of life. The value of adjunctive psychotherapies is recognized in *Kaplan & Sadock's Comprehensive Textbook of Psychiatry*: "These adjunctive psychotherapeutic approaches have now been demonstrated as efficacious in multiple randomized trials and should be considered as a fundamental phase of treatment." (Sadock & Sadock, 2005, p. 1672)

An early study by Susan Cochran (1984) illustrated the power of brief targeted psychoeducational techniques. In a small but impressive randomly controlled trial with 14 patients, she demonstrated that a brief individual six-session CBT supplement to standard care significantly increased medication compliance at 6-month follow-up and reduced the likelihood of hospitalization or treatment discontinuation.

Another small randomized, controlled trial at Massachusetts General Hospital (Hirschfield et al., 1998) of an 11-session group-based CBT model demonstrated that patients treated through CBT had significantly longer periods of normal mood and fewer affective episodes than a control group receiving medication alone.

Perry et al. (1999) compared outcomes for 69 bipolar patients randomly assigned to a 7–12 session individual CBT (plus routine care) versus routine care alone. Compared to routine care alone, patients in the CBT plus routine care demonstrated an increased period of relapse-free functioning before their first manic episode (65 weeks on average for the treatment group versus 17 weeks for routine care).

Lam et al. (2000) compared randomized assignment to routine care plus 12–20 sessions of CBT versus routine care for 25 bipolar outpatients. Treatment with CBT was associated with significant reductions in hypomanic and total bipolar episodes at 6 and 12 months. In a striking finding at 1-year follow-up, 10 of the 12 patients treated with CBT experienced no bipolar episodes, compared with only 2 of 11 patients assigned to usual care.

Frank et al. (1997) developed interpersonal and social rhythm therapy (IPSRT), an enhanced form of interpersonal therapy for patients with bipolar I disorder, with the goal of establishing regularity in social routines. When compared with a medication clinic, subjects assigned to IPSRT demonstrated significantly greater stability in daily routines with increasing time in treatment. On the other hand, subjects assigned to the medication clinic condition showed essentially no change in the stability of their social routines. The study concludes that IPSRT may be capable of influencing lifestyle regularity in patients with bipolar I disorder and possibly protect patients against future manic and depressive episodes.

Scott, Garland, and Moorhead (2001) compared 42 patients with bipolar disorder receiving CBT to a waiting list comparison group. At 6-month follow-up, CBT patients demonstrated significantly greater improvements in overall functioning and reductions in depressive symptoms. In an 18-month follow-up of 29 patients, relapse rates were 60% below baseline levels (18 months prior to treatment).

Miklowitz et al. (2003) compared 30 bipolar patients after acute episodes who were assigned to up to 50 sessions of family-focused treatment (FFT) to 70 patients who had received standard community care. Patients in the FFT condition had a longer survival interval (time without relapse) and showed greater reductions in depressive symptoms over baseline levels at one year.

In a more recent and larger study, Colom et al. (2003) compared randomized assignment of 120 bipolar patients to 21 sessions of group psychoeducation (plus standard care) against 21 sessions of unstructured group meetings (plus standard care). Group psychoeducation significantly reduced the number of relapses per subject and increased the survival time to depressed, manic, and mixed episodes, as well as the number and length of hospitalizations.

In another large randomized trial, Lam et al. (2003) compared treatment as usual to 12–18 sessions of CBT for 103 bipolar patients in a randomized clinical trial. Specialized CBT involved information and education, identification of prodromal symptoms and development of coping plans, and management of sleep and routines. Patients assigned to the CBT condition over the 12-month period had significantly fewer bipolar episodes, days in a bipolar episode, and number of bipolar admissions, improved psychosocial functioning, and the less self-reported mood symptoms.

In a summary review of 40 randomized controlled studies with serious mental illness including schizophrenia and bipolar disorder, Mueser et al. (2002) conclude: "Although some studies of coping skills training differed in the symptoms they targeted, they all employed time-limited, cognitive-behavioral interventions. Thus psychoeducation, behavioral tailoring for medication, training in relapse prevention, and coping skills training employing cognitive-behavioral techniques are strongly supported components of illness management." (p. 1280).

In another recent review of psychosocial interventions specifically for bipolar disorder, Zaretsky (2003) concludes as follows: "In summary, individual CBT in bipolar disorder appears to be the most broadly effective of bipolar psychosocial interventions in both open and controlled trials ... Psychoeducational interventions appear to improve medication compliance and should be considered early in the course of the illness. Treatment interventions that focus on helping patients identify early prodromes of relapse in order to take proactive steps have also been shown to be effective." (p. 85).

Gutierrez and Scott (2004) note that certain interventions appear to be more effective for bipolar depression (IPSRT and family-focused treatment), while others seem to target both manic and depressive episodes (CBT). In their summary of randomized controlled trials of psychosocial treatment for bipolar disorder, Gutierrez and Scott conclude: "Positive outcomes include increased medication adherence, improved attitudes towards and knowledge about treatments, decreased number and length of hospitalizations, fewer relapses or extended symptom-free periods, improved social functioning, increased work productivity, improved sense of well-being improved family functioning, and improved marital relationships." (p. 96).

4.4   Variations and Combinations of Methods

This section highlights specialized approaches to the treatment of bipolar disorder, including (a) family-based treatment and family management and (b) self-help approaches incorporating the recovery model in the long-term management of bipolar disorder.

4.4.1   Family-Based Treatment and Family Management

A number of studies have confirmed that a majority of discharged psychiatric patients return home to live with family members. In many cases, the ultimate burden of serious mental illness falls on the family. Family-based approaches, including family psychoeducation programs, may be the most underutilized evidence-based interventions in the treatment of bipolar disorder and other serious mental illnesses. The term "family psychoeducation" should be viewed broadly as including a number of both educational and therapeutic interven-

Table 26
**Principles for Working with Families: Critical Elements for Family Interventions
for Individuals with Serious Mental Illness (adapted from Dixon et al., 2001)**

- Coordinate all elements of treatment and rehabilitation to ensure that everyone is working towards the same goals in a collaborative, supportive relationship.
- Pay attention to the social as well as the clinical needs of the consumer.
- Provide optimum medication management.
- Listen to families' concerns and involve them as equal partners in the planning and delivery of treatment.
- Assess strengths and weaknesses in the family ability to support the consumer.
- Address feelings of loss.
- Provide relevant information for the consumer and his or her family at appropriate times.
- Provide an explicit crisis plan and response.
- Help improve communication among family members.
- Provide training for the family in structured problem-solving techniques.
- Encourage family members to expand their social support networks- for example, to participate in family support organizations such as NAMI.
- Be flexible in meeting the needs of the family.
- Provide the family with easy access to another professional in the event that the current work with the family ceases.

tions. In an overview of research on family-based interventions, Dixon, McFarlane, and Lefley (2001) conclude: "Studies have shown markedly higher reductions in relapse and rehospitalizations rates among consumers whose families received psychoeducation than among those who received individual services." (p. 904). Furthermore, reductions in relapse rates were higher for programs lasting more than 3 months, and in order to be effective these programs needed to include "skills training, ongoing guidance about management of mental illness, and emotional support for family members" (p. 905).

Some of the critical elements of family intervention as applied to schizophrenia are listed in Table 26, as developed in a 1998 World Schizophrenia Fellowship conference and identified by Dixon et al. (2001). While these principles were developed primarily for work with families with individuals with schizophrenia, we suggest that many of the same principles and intervention strategies appear to be similarly effective with bipolar disorder and represent a useful working framework for working with families in general.

Miklowitz and colleagues (1988) have specifically demonstrated that individuals with bipolar disorder returning from the hospital to stressful family environments are at higher risk for relapse and rehospitalizations. The goal of family-based treatment approaches is to reduce levels of high expressed emotion (negative, critical, over-involved emotionally, or highly conflictual interactions) in the family. Key objectives (also identified in Chapter 2) in Miklowitz and Goldstein's family-based approach, Family-Focused Treatment (FFT) (Miklowitz & Goldstein, 1997) are as follows:

**Family stress
contributes to
relapse in bipolar
disorder**

- Help patient and family members integrate experiences with bipolar disorder
- Assist patient/family members in accepting vulnerability to future episodes

Family management interventions are targeted to reduce stress

- Assist patient/family members in accepting ongoing need for medication
- Help patient/family members differentiate between effects of bipolar disorder and patient's personality
- Assist patient/family members in recognizing and coping with stressful events (likely to trigger new episodes)
- Help family reestablish functional relationships

We think it is useful to conceptualize family treatment using Miklowitz's and Goldstein's model (Miklowitz, 2002; Miklowitz & Goldstein, 1997), which defines three main phases of treatment – a psychoeducational phase, a communication skills training phase, and a problem-solving phase – and adds a final maintenance phase including ongoing crisis intervention and relapse prevention.

Families experience intense disorganization, guilt and self-blame that is destabilizing

During an individual's initial episode of serious mental illness, families are likely to experience disorganization, demoralization, and intense guilt and self-blame that can be experienced as absolutely destabilizing and disastrous for family members. The goal in this phase is to provide information and support to the patient and family members, offering a realistic understanding of bipolar disorder and a rationale for treatment that provides hope for the future. This will involve, at minimum, helping family members understand the ongoing role of medication in treatment, identify specific symptoms of bipolar disorder, identify warning signs of impending episodes, and develop a shared understanding of the basic treatment approaches identified in Chapter 4: Treatment above, including mood monitoring, identifying prodromes of illness, and developing coping plans. We routinely provide Dr. Miklowitz's excellent book, *The Bipolar Disorder Survival Guide – What You and Your Family Need to Know* to families and always receive enthusiastic responses. This often leads to useful discussions of protective and risk factors, a "what's me versus what's the disorder" debate, appropriate family concerns versus intrusive overprotectiveness, and the role of self-management.

After initial assessment meetings, which should always involve family members (see Section 1.7) and psychoeducational sessions, it is often useful to meet individually with the patient for several sessions to develop a strong therapeutic alliance and an initial treatment plan focusing on monitoring and

Agenda for initial sessions with the family

Table 27
Sample Agenda for Initial Family Sessions

- Set goal of supporting family and keeping patient stable.
- Explain the rationale for ongoing treatment with medication as well as psychotherapy.
- Reduce blaming and guilt – everyone is dong the best they can.
- Identify early warning signs.
- Develop a specific plan about how best to monitor warning signs (who is responsible for what).
- Help the patient identify "helpful things family members can do."
- Help the patient identify "unhelpful things family members should avoid doing."
- Develop an action plan for relapses.

identifying early warning signs. This plan can then be shared with family members, and family members can jointly develop a list of agreed upon "Warning signs" in a collaborative fashion with the patient and the therapist.

The goal is to limit this list to specific warning signs of manic and depressive episodes and to avoid general behaviors that may be the focus of family conflict but are nonspecific to bipolar disorder. Frequently, in adolescents and young adults, conflicts about increasing autonomy and independence can become intermingled with concerns about the symptoms of bipolar disorder (especially mania and hypomania). It can be useful to differentiate high-risk behaviors with a potential for harm or serious consequences from annoying or irritating behaviors that are unpleasant but not life-threatening.

In the example presented in Table 28 below, after several individual sessions with the patient, the therapist met with the family and collaboratively developed a list of agreed-upon early warning signs. The therapist worked to prioritize high-risk behaviors where family members could readily agree on health or safety risks from other behaviors that did not pose an imminent hazard. The intent of this exercise is not to come up with the perfect list, but to establish a cooperative and collaborative framework in which family members work together toward mutually acceptable goals for treatment. Unresolved items are best deferred for further discussion, keeping the focus on areas of agreement. Indeed, in this instance, the family could not agree on some items (starred in the table) which were left for further discussion.

Helping the patient and family identify early warning signs

Finally, when excessive monitoring of possible bipolar symptoms causes conflict between family members and the patient, it is useful to reframe the familys' occasional intrusiveness or excessive concern as a natural response of caring parents to a very serious illness. This creates a possible framework for further discussion of what is a more optimal level of concern and monitoring. The vignette below addresses balancing family concern for possible symptoms and high-risk behaviors with excessive intrusiveness that can be viewed as a threat to autonomy by adolescents and young adults.

Problems with parental worry and over monitoring

Because many of the interventions described in the main treatment chapter can be applied in a family context, we will not repeat material from that section but instead offer a few selected vignettes to give a flavor of how to adapt individual procedures to fit into a family treatment model. For example,

---

Table 28
Identifying Warning Signs Collaboratively in a Family Context

- Sleeping less than 4 hours a night
- Withdrawing from classes
- Rushing to make up and losing sleep
- "I can do anything" energy – excessive multitasking
- Unable to concentrate on studies
- Always feeling angry
- Driving recklessly
- Drinking too much
- Reversed sleep cycle – too tired to attend class
- Pressure to get things right away
- Inviting certain friends over the family doesn't approve of

it is useful to use "unhelpful thought records" for identifying and resolving problematic responses to family interactions that may be a factor in precipitating episodes of mania or depression. In these thought records – which can best be developed in conjoint family interviews – we tend to emphasize the interpersonal context of the individual's behaviors and point out chains of interactions and responses that are problematic or maladaptive. Additionally, this helps family members develop empathy, and more fully understand and appreciate the internal experience of the identified patient and identify unhelpful responses and interactions. Attempt to do this in a "no-blame" framework, with the understanding that everyone in the family is doing the best they can to cope with a highly stressful, destabilizing situation. For example, the following vignettes illustrate the use of standard cognitive therapy strategies and then adapting them to address the interpersonal, familial context in a way that is helpful to all family members and reinforces more adaptive communication and behavioral patterns.

Clinical vignette: Cognitive therapy in an interpersonal family context

Clinical Vignette
"Why Are You Sleeping So Much? Are You OK?"

Andrea, a very bright and high-achieving 21-year-old college student, returned to live at home after a serious period of depression followed by a manic episode in her first year at college. During her manic episode Andrea had engaged in a number of behaviors that were frightening and disturbing both to her and to her family. As a result, her mother was particularly concerned and attempted to closely monitor changes in her behavior, including any significant changes in sleep and wake cycles and other behavioral changes associated with the onset of hypomania and mania. In the mother's view, there would be realistically disastrous consequences for failing to identify signs of instability that might indicate the emergence of new symptoms. Unfortunately, this sometimes resulted in a high level of conflict between mother and daughter. Whenever Andrea felt criticized by her mother, she tended to experience episodes of depression that were destabilizing and interfered with her functioning at college.

During a conjoint family therapy session in the first eight weeks of therapy, Andrea reported that she had become severely dejected and depressed because she felt that her mother thought she was a "lazy" person. This resulted in her staying in bed throughout the day and missing several of her scheduled activities, resulting in her feeling significantly more depressed. In the thought record summarized in Table 29, the therapist attempted to illustrate the "downward spiral" into depression that occurred in the context of concerns expressed by the mother which were experienced by the daughter as both critical and intrusive.

The therapist attempted to help Andrea develop countering thoughts (also illustrated in Table 29) that would assist her in feeling less criticized and disrupt some of her negative self-labeling, and pointed out her tendency to sabotage herself by missing classes and other important activities when she felt criticized. This resulted in a serious "downward spiral," in which minor criticisms were perceived as major threats to self-esteem and precipitated further withdrawal, isolation, and self-blaming. The final outcome was that what might have started out as a relatively minor setback became a much more serious depressive episode that interfered with daily functioning and threatened important longer-term goals.

Table 29
Thought Record: "I'm a Lazy Person Staying in Bed All Day"

Situation	I'm trying to nap and mom says, "Get up, you've been watching TV all day."
Thoughts	• I'm lazy • I don't care about my future • I'm less of a person (95%) • I'm not motivated • I'm not good enough (99%) • If mom thinks I'm lazy than I must be lazy (90%) • I am bad person • Whatever my mom says about me is true. • My thoughts and feelings are not valid.
Feelings	• Dejected • Depressed • Irritable • Annoyed • Sensitive • [Anxious]
Behaviors	• Stay in bed more ("my escape") [avoidance] • Avoids studies [Self-sabotaging behaviors] • Loss of focus on goals (feels worse) • Difficulty scheduling, as schedule has become less structured
Alternative Thoughts	• If I really was a lazy person I wouldn't be trying this hard in school. • If I was lazy I wouldn't care about spending time with friends. • If I was lazy why would I attend school, I would be skipping classes. • My friend tells me I'm important, therefore I do make a difference. • Other friends see my ideas as valuable.

Clinical Dialogue: "Plugging" Individual Cognitive Work into the Family Interaction

Clinical Vignette
Reducing Family Conflict over Excessive Monitoring

Patient: There are still times when she'll [the mother] think I'm sleeping too much. Then, I see her reading the "Bipolar Book" [*The Bipolar Disorder Survival Guide* by David Miklowitz] right when I wake up. And that gets me stressed out.

Therapist: That's like waving the red flag?

Patient: Yes.

Therapist: Let's go back to where we left off last week. I think we identified a kind of interaction between the two of you where you [mother] become concerned and there are a lot of reminders and cues you give to make sure that your daughter is "on track." And then you [daughter] get very irritated and it kind of ends up in a very angry explosive incident.

Clinical dialogue: Helping the family reduce conflict

Patient: It's not helpful. I read in the book that stress causes more problems.
Therapist: Yeah. I think we came to the conclusion that this wasn't really working for either of you; that it was backfiring and making things less stable. So one big goal here is to get the two of you working together in a way that doesn't create such a high level of conflict. We would like to meet each of your goals without increased conflict. Is that right?
Mother: Yes, I'm frustrated, so frustrated.
Daughter: Yes.
Therapist: So we had an experiment going to see how things would go without any reminders about medication or mood graphing last week. How did things go? Were you able to get on the same page?
Patient: Well, sometimes she had to remind me and other times I did it on my own. But with the medication I definitely had that covered. She didn't have to remind me at all.
Therapist: Did she remind you?
Patient: No. I know that's what I should be doing anyway.
Therapist: Is the medication an area that the two of you are succeeding in?
Patient: Yeah.
Therapist: So let's start there. Why is that working for you?
Patient: It's just ingrained; especially since the fact that my mom doesn't remind me anymore. Sometimes [in the past] I wanted to not take medication because of the things she'll say. Right before I get a chance to take the medication she'll remind me. It makes me want to rebel.
Therapist: So medication is an area you have been successful in, following through and doing it yourself. Have you missed doses or days in the past 2 weeks?
Patient: No.
Therapist: To me this is an example of what is working.
Mother: Yeah.
Therapist: It seems like it's working – you're able to not worry about it too much and stay clear, and that's helping her.
Mother: Yeah.
Therapist: And the outcome is what?
Mother: She's taking it [the medication].
Therapist: And how does that affect your relationship with your daughter?
Mother: It's more positive. I don't say a thing and she just does it.
Therapist: So the outcome is positive here and you feel less worried?
Mother: Yeah. I really appreciate her taking her medication.
Therapist: So you have a more positive relationship in this area and that encourages you [daughter] to take more responsibility and feel good about doing it yourself. And that helps you [mother] not feel too worried. So this is a good model. How could we take this success and apply it to other areas where you are still having problems? We all agree this is good outcome where you feel less conflict, right? You feel less angry and frustrated, right?
Mother and daughter: Hmm.
Therapist: Does this sound like I'm getting it right here?
Daughter: Definitely.

Over the course of several months of therapy, where several similar interactional patterns were reviewed, the relationship between mother and daughter greatly improved and the daughter became increasingly independent and self-sufficient, eventually planning a return to college and independent living.

4.4.2.   Self-Help Approaches Incorporating the Recovery Model

Integrating Evidence-Based Treatment and the Recovery Model

It would be impossible to begin discussion of recovery from bipolar disorder without reference to the profound impact that Kay Jamison has had, both on our understanding and conceptualization of this disorder and on our hopefulness about the ability of patients to recover from the most severe episodes of illness and rebuild meaning and purpose in their lives. As Dr. Jamison noted in her introduction to *Manic-Depressive Illness*: "Manic-depressive illness magnifies common human experiences to larger than life proportions. Among its symptoms are exaggerations of normal sadness and fatigue, joy and exuberance, sensuality and sexuality, irritability and rage, energy and creativity." (Goodwin & Jamison, 1990, p. 3)

The recovery model and the role of self-help

We take the view that patients can recover from severe illness and that the heart of recovery is rediscovering meaning and purpose, not just the amelioration of psychiatric symptoms or the stabilization of mood. What is the point of merely being "well," if life has no meaning or purpose? As Bill Anthony has indicated in his vision of the meaning of recovery, "Recovery involves the development of new meaning and purpose in one's life as one grows beyond the catastrophic effects of mental illness" (Anthony & Spaniol, 1994, p. 527). As we interviewed a group of patients who had been stable for over 2 years, a constant theme emerged that bipolar disorder was becoming simply one facet of a rich, varied, and interesting life, and having the disorder was no longer viewed as an overwhelming threat or disaster. As one patient put it quite graphically: "Recovery means not waking up in the morning and having your first thought be, 'Oh shit! I have bipolar disorder.' Instead I find myself thinking about what I am going to do today."

The role of meaning and personal values

As illustrated in Table 30, this broader view of the disorder and the meaning of recovery can be integrated into our clinical work by emphasizing the importance of self-management and the need to make a lifelong commitment to get well and stay well.

Integrating recovery principles with evidence-based care

Table 30
Integrating Evidence-based Treatment and the Recovery Model: First Principles

- Treatment is a collaborative enterprise.
- Accept the patient as the most important resource in therapy and learn from the patient's experience, strengths, and past efforts in resolving problems.
- Teach patients the skills they need to manage their health-related problems.
- Treatment goals are ultimately defined by the patient.
- Don't forget "big picture" treatment goals:
  - Increased independence
  - Increased responsibility
  - Satisfying relationships
  - Good quality of life
- Providing opportunities for housing, education and employment.
- Feeling useful and finding purposeful activities that make life meaningful.

The following sections describe some key areas that are likely to be addressed in relationship to guilt, shame stigma, hopelessness, and the need to work toward "remoralizing" the patient.

Basic Skills: Addressing Stigmatizing Thoughts – Helping Patients with Guilt and Shame Over Episodes

It is almost axiomatic that patients with bipolar disorder suffer from guilt and shame over their behavior in past manic and hypomanic episodes. While bipolar disorder has a variable course, manic episodes often end with the emergence of an acute depressive phase. Depression is often compounded by excessive guilt and shame over risk-taking and pleasure-seeking behaviors associated with the manic phase. Use of automatic thought records can be helpful in addressing some of the cognitive distortions for patients who suffer from excessive shame and guilt during dysthymic or depressed periods.

Clinical Vignette
"I Called My Mother Names"

During periods of depression, Frederick often ruminated about bad behavior during past manic episodes. He was particularly upset by an incident in which he had been very rude to his mother during an irritable manic phase shortly prior to her death. Bill often replayed this and other incidents in his head over and over again, becoming progressively more depressed, ashamed, and guilty. During these periods he would isolate himself and withdraw socially, which further contributed to his depression. He continued to worry about this long after his mood stabilized and he no longer appeared to be in danger of a manic episode due to continued pharmacotherapy and psychotherapy.

This ongoing guilt was addressed in a group therapy intervention in which Frederick discussed shameful acts that he was concerned about group members who shared many of his feelings and concerns. The therapist then asked Frederick to write down the most distressing thoughts: How could I have done that (spoken rudely to his aging mother)?" "I could lose important relationships or damage them if it happens again." Frederick was able to review some of the unhelpful behaviors (isolation, withdrawal, attempts to avoid these painful thoughts) that resulted in increased distress and depression and develop more helpful responses (contacting others). As a result of this exercise, he was also able to develop a more compassionate view of his illness and a more motivating helpful view of what he could do to stay stable (see Table 31).

Combating Social Stigma

In a chapter summarizing a dialogue between psychiatrists and "consumer-practitioners," Blanch, Fisher, Tucker Walsh and Chassman (1997, p. 70) make the following observations: "'Recovery' relates not only to the experience of symptoms, but also to the secondary assaults of stigma, discrimination and abuse: One person noted 'Dealing with internalized stigma was almost as difficult and took as much away from my life as the symptoms did' ... Hope is perhaps the most fundamental factor in recovery" (p. 70).

Patients with bipolar disorder are exposed to real world discrimination and stigmatization in healthcare, insurance, social and job settings. It is not surpris-

Table 31
Unhelpful Thought Record: Guilt and self-Blame over Past Manic Episodes

Event	Memories of being manic or delusional (when alone, isolated, or bored)
Negative Automatic Thoughts	"How could I have done that?" "I could lose important relationships or damage them if it happens again."
Feelings (rating of intensity 0–100%)	Ashamed 50% Fear 50% Shameful/Bad Regret 50% Horrified
Thinking Errors	Mind-reading All or nothing thinking
Unhelpful Behaviors	Avoids thoughts
More Helpful Behaviors	Call siblings
Countering Thoughts	"I'm an unfortunate person." "I can take steps to protect myself and others." "I've been successful at being stable for a number of years."

ing that hopelessness, stigma, and demoralization are profound problems for individuals with this disorder. The following vignette addresses interventions that target some of the core issues that contribute to ongoing demoralization and reinforce negative schema.

Table 32
Thought Record: Developing Coping Strategies for Shame and Social Embarrassment

Event	Person from my past showed up
Thoughts	He remembers me. He's wondering how I am now. He saw me when I was really depressed.
Feelings	Fearful Ashamed Shame
Thinking Error	(Projection, Mind-reading)
Responses	Withdrawal and avoiding others
Alternative/Adaptive thoughts	I'm okay now. What's on my mind is not necessarily on their mind. I have a disorder just like mom. I am on a medication regimen that works and I am doing the right thing.
Coping strategies	Actively deal with the problem!

Clinical Vignette

Avoiding Social Activity and Family Gatherings

Even though Sally was stable and no longer experiencing acute manic episodes, she found herself increasingly isolated and withdrawn. She found it difficult to deal with social situations, especially when she was at risk of meeting people from her past who might be aware of some of her embarrassing behavior associated with past episodes of mania. During a recent family gathering, Sally had felt especially depressed and ashamed when she encountered a person "from her past." This situation was reviewed using an "Unhelpful Thought Record" to help Sally deal with some of her embarrassed anxious feelings to identify and reinforce more adaptive coping responses.

Remoralizing the Patient

Bipolar disorder is an unforgiving illness that provides patients with many cycles of depression and mania, resulting in severe demoralization over time. Patients experience helplessness and hopelessness in that their best past efforts to avoid or reduce mood swings have often failed. Continued cycles of mania and depression often have devastating effects on family members, significant others, finances, and work. A number of studies that have reviewed the longitudinal course of bipolar disorder have concluded that patients spend a majority of their time in a moderately to significantly depressed state, with significant impairments in functioning, even if they are not in a severe episode. Much of the disability associated with this disorder results from these long periods of subsyndromal depression and dysthmia, perhaps more so than the effects of acute manic episodes, however dramatic.

Combating Demoralization And Hopelessness

One of the first goals of therapy is to address hopelessness and demoralization. Often patients are initially unable to follow through on homework assignments and other tasks because of a pervasive sense of hopelessness and demoralization.

A primary and ongoing task of therapy is to instill hope and to give the patient a realistic level of confidence that they can hope to experience better times ahead, although they may be feeling severely depressed currently. "Tunnel vision," specifically an inability to see a more positive future, a constriction of imagined possibilities, is a symptom of depression that often interferes with the ability to accept or benefit from treatment. The case below illustrates strategies of addressing hopelessness and demoralization.

Clinical Vignette

Combating Demoralization and Hopelessness

Tanya, a 22-year-old Asian-American woman, began therapy during an episode of severe depression in which she often felt "numb," immobilized, and unable to "get going", to the extent that she stayed in bed for several days at a time. During these periods she also experienced a strong sense of depersonalization in which she felt "robotic" and experienced her thinking as "muddle-headed."

Although very bright and with an advanced degree in engineering, she was reduced to doing project-oriented consulting and felt that her last project had been an abysmal failure. Because she felt so panicky and incompetent at work, she assumed that she was viewed as grossly incompetent and would never be offered another consulting project. After several initial sessions, Tanya agreed to schedule several pleasant events that involved increasing her social contacts and getting her out of bed. One of the consequences of depression is to reduce positive events in the individual's life because of withdrawal and social isolation. Depression can become a downward spiral where lowered mood results in reduced activity levels, and reduced activity levels reduce any opportunities for pleasure and add to the progression of depression. The goal of assigning pleasant events for patients who are depressed is to help activate them and develop some opportunities for positive reinforcement.

When she returned for the next session, Tanya reported that she had been unable to follow through on any of the agreed-upon assignments and reported feeling increasingly depressed. A cognitive therapy intervention was used in which we examined the thoughts she was having that seemed to be associated with feeling hopeless, apathetic, and unmotivated. A "Thought Record," also known as a "Dysfunctional Thought Record" or an "Unhelpful Thought Record," is designed to help patients evaluate their thinking process and identify distortions, thinking "errors," or unhelpful thoughts. Patients are asked to review their thoughts, identify possible thinking errors, and then develop more helpful rational responses. We discussed her difficulty following through on these assignments and developed a Thought Record (see Table 33) reflecting the automatic thoughts and the feelings she experienced when she was considering her homework tasks. Note that prior to doing this exercise, the patient had been asked to read *The Feeling Good Handbook* by David Burns (for details, see Appendix 8). This book is an excellent reference for patients to become acquainted with basic cognitive therapy skills, and is especially useful for patients who are depressed and having problems with avoidance and procrastination.

Tanya reported feeling very apathetic, numb, doubtful and hopeless in conjunction with these thoughts. After identifying some of the cognitive distortions associated with these thoughts, Tanya proceeded to develop the following more rational responses in Table 34 below. It took some time for Tanya to come up with alternative ways of thinking. Even though it may be time-consuming to wait for severely depressed patients to think through this type of exercise, it is important to let patients come up with their own analysis and suggested alternate responses rather than having the therapist "fill in the blanks".

At the end of the exercise, Tanya reexamined her feelings and decided that she felt more hopeful and less doubtful and anxious when considering her homework tasks for the following week.

It should be noted that for patients like Tanya who are severely depressed, one exercise is unlikely to have a lasting impact and multiple efforts will need to be made over time to address hopelessness and demoralization. In fact, after 2–3 weeks of feeling significantly better, Tanya returned to therapy after a 2 week break unable to do her homework and feeling very hopeless again. She began the session with the statement, "I feel like I took a nosedive", and she rated her mood as −3 on a +5 to −5 scale. She had not followed through on homework and had the following thoughts:

"I don't really care anymore about making an effort, because it won't make a difference."

"I want to crawl in a hole and not deal with the world right now."

"I'm frustrated that I made an improvement and slid back."

"When I make progress, there's always some glitch; something bad happens."

These thoughts left her feeling numb, blank, and hopeless. She noticed several thinking errors, including "emotional reasoning" ("I feel like it won't make a difference, therefore, it won't make a difference") predicting the future, overgeneralization, magnifying problems, and minimizing positives ("When I make progress, something bad *always* happens"). With some effort she was able to come up with several countering thoughts:

"I am feeling more hopeful about my therapy."

"Things don't always stay bad; I have felt better in the past."

"Even if I do slide back, I'm getting help and have good support systems."

At the end of this exercise the patient felt somewhat less hopeless and rated her mood as a −1 or −2 on the +5 to −5 scale. This may seem to be only modest progress, but in an additive fashion these small steps help the patient move forward.

Using thought records to address hopelessness

Table 33
Addressing Demoralization and Hopelessness

Automatic Thoughts	Possible Thinking Errors
"Don't feel like doing them. It seems silly."	All-or-nothing thinking; over-generalization, Jumping to conclusions
"It won't be useful or change anything."	Overgeneralization; all-or-nothing thinking
"I'll be too robotic."	Jumping to conclusions
"I'll be disappointed anyway, so why bother."	Jumping to conclusions

Identifying thinking errors for hopeless patients

Developing rational responses to hopeless thoughts

Table 34
Addressing Demoralization and Hopelessness – Rational Responses

Automatic Thoughts	Rational Responses
"I don't feel like doing them. It seems silly."	Unable to come up with response.
"It won't be useful or change anything."	Unable to come up with response.
"I'll be too robotic."	"Even so, it's better than doing nothing."
"I'll be disappointed anyway, so why bother."	"Maybe I will be disappointed, but I might not be 100% disappointed."

Hopelessness is also a key countertransference issue for therapists working with severely depressed, demoralized, hopeless or suicidal patients. It is important not to become enmeshed in the patient's sense of powerlessness and hopelessness and not to accept their biased view of their abilities and opportunities for improvement.

The Role of Self-Help and Support Groups

For maintenance of gains in long-term recovery of bipolar disorder and other serious mental illnesses, the clinician must look outside the framework of traditional treatment and help the patient become actively involved in self-help support groups. Many of the patients we have treated who have been most successful have developed ongoing support systems, in part through participating in organized self-help groups. Active participation in self-help groups reflects the same active self-management efforts that are a key to long-term illness management and recovery. There are a number of well-organized and dedicated organizations (see Appendix 8) that offer a variety of education and supportive services targeted to individuals with a serious mental illness and their families. These groups provide extremely helpful education, social support, and help to destigmatize the illness in ways that are not available to the professional therapist.

The role of self-help and support groups in recovery

4.5   Problems in Carrying out the Treatment

In addition to ample clinical challenges, there are a number of known risks that the clinician will want to be familiar with when treating individuals with bipolar disorder. In this section we highlight three key issues: suicide risk and management, treatment adherence (specifically, taking medications as prescribed), and comorbid substance misuse.

Key treatment risks

Table 35
Special Problems in the Treatment of Bipolar Disorder

- Significantly higher risk for completed suicide (15%) and suicide attempts (25%–50%) (Goodwin & Jamison, 1990)
- Low rates of treatment adherence – specifically following prescribed medication regimens (Goodwin & Jamison, 1990; Hilty, Brady, & Hales 1999)
- Misuse of alcohol or illegal drugs (estimated at 60%) significantly increases suicide risk (Hilty et al., 1999)

4.5.1   Suicide Risk Assessment and Management

Suicide risk is the most serious clinical consideration in treating patients with bipolar disorder. It has been estimated that between 25% and 50% of patients with bipolar disorder will make a lifetime suicide attempt and that 8.6% to 18.9% will die due to completed suicide (Goodwin & Jamison, 1990). The likelihood of a suicide attempt in bipolar disorder is higher than that in any other axis I disorder, including major depression. The odds ratio for a lifetime history of any suicide attempt according to the National Comorbidity Study (Kessler, Borges, & Walters, 1999) was 29.7, indicating that patients with bipolar disorder are almost 30 times more likely to attempt suicide than a nonclinical population. In a summary of 15 studies, the APA Practice Guidelines determined that the risk for completed suicide in bipolar disorder was 15 times higher than the expected mortality rate in a nonclinical population. A second consideration is the fact that bipolar illness is also associated with a high risk of comorbid substance abuse, which is itself a risk factor for suicide.

Suicide assessment and risk management

Suicide Risk Factors

Leverich, Altshuler, and Frye (2003), in a review of suicide risk, note several other factors common to bipolar disorder that have been linked to suicide risk, including the following: comorbid anxiety disorder or extreme psychic agitation, panic, dysphoric mania (where depressive symptoms are prominent during a manic episode), a history of drug and alcohol misuse, the occurrence of negative life events, and the absence of social supports.

In one prospective study that followed a sample of 307 patients with bipolar I or bipolar II disorder for 7 years, 42% were found to have made a suicide attempt at some point in their lives (Slama, Belliver, Henry, Rousseva, Etain, Rouillon, & Leboyer, 2004). Slama et al. (2004) identified the following factors associated with a risk of attempted suicide in a sample of bipolar I and bipolar II patients:

- Early onset of the illness
- Total number of depressive episodes
- Total number of major mood episodes
- History of antidepressant-induced mania
- Familial history of suicidal behavior

In a review of suicide risk in a sample of 648 patients with bipolar I or bipolar II disorder in the Stanley Foundation Bipolar Network, Leverich et al. (2003) determined that 34% of their sample reported a history of suicide attempts. Suicide attempts were associated with the following risk factors:

- Early physical abuse
- Early sexual abuse
- Family history of suicide attempts and substance abuse
- Higher levels of Axis I and II (cluster B) comorbidity
- A pattern of increasing severity of mania
- Greater number (>4) of prior hospitalizations for depression
- More reported suicidal thoughts when manic and when depressed
- Lack of a confidant or death of a significant other

Leverich et al. (2003) conclude as follows: "More vigorous treatment of the depressive phases of bipolar disorder, which are 3 times more prevalent than manic episodes in general and are especially prominent in those patients with a history of suicide attempts in particular, would also appear to be an important avenue of pursuit."

Angst, Sellaro, and Angst (1998) determined that in bipolar and major depressive disorders the risk for completed suicide was reduced from a rate of 29.2% for those not in treatment to 6.4% for those in treatment. The clinician must conclude also that aggressive treatment, especially emphasizing early intervention and targeting depressive symptoms and dysphoria, is life saving and of critical importance in reducing mortality and morbidity in patients with bipolar I and bipolar II disorders.

This section will now address general guidelines for assessment of suicide risk, generally accepted practices in managing risk, and specific applications to patients with bipolar disorder.

Suicide risk, specifically making a severe suicide attempt, is associated mainly with severe episodes of depression and dysphoric states in bipolar I and II disorder and not with manic or hypomanic states. It follows that many of the strategies used to intervene in major depression to address hopelessness (dysphoria and demoralization) will also be effective in addressing suicide risk in the bipolar population.

Assessment of Clinical Risk Factors for Suicide: General Risk Factors

The following discussion is based on the American Psychiatric Association (APA) *Practice Guidelines For the Treatment of Psychiatric Disorders* (APA, 2004) which can be viewed as a consensus document illustrating best practices in suicide risk management.

Assessment of general risk factors for suicide

In addressing and managing acute immediate suicide risk, the clinician will have a two-fold task:

1. Identify specific factors/features that increase or decrease risk of suicide and that are subject to psychological/psychiatric interventions.
2. Address the patient's immediate safety and determine the most appropriate interventions/treatment settings.

The clinician's most immediate task will be to assess the presence of suicidal or self-harming thoughts, plans, behaviors, and intent. This assessment will need to include a specific consideration of methods that the patient is considering, including the lethality of the method, expectations about lethality, and the degree to which the chosen means is immediately accessible. The interview should also explore the frequency, intensity, timing, and persistence of suicidal ideation. If current suicidal ideation is present, the clinician should explore in detail the presence of a specific plan for suicide, including any steps taken to enact plans or prepare for death.

If the patient reports a specific method, it is important to find out more about his or her expectations about the lethality of the method. As a general rule, if the actual lethality of the method exceeds the patient's expectation, then risk of accidental suicide will be higher. Assessment of lethality will depend on how detailed and specific the patient's suicide plan is, to what extent an especially violent and irreversible method is preferred, and finally the strength of the patient's intent to die. When interviewing after a suicide attempt, it is important to ask the patient if she or he is relieved or disappointed that the attempt failed and if any significant predisposing circumstances have changed since the attempt. Patients who signal that they are disappointed should be viewed as at high immediate risk of a second attempt.

Assessing lethality and removing lethal means

Importance of documentation and consultation

Table 36:
Risk Management Considerations in Managing Suicide Risk (adapted from APA, 2004)

- Documentation of suicide assessment is essential.
- If patient has access to a firearm, therapist must restrict and secure access by assuring that this and other weapons are removed. Specific recommendations about removal of firearms or other weapons must also be documented.
- Communications with supervisors, consultants, family members, and significant others must also be carefully documented.
- Consultation with other mental health professionals is highly recommended.

The presence of hopelessness, impulsiveness, anhedonia, panic attacks, or anxiety in conjunction with suicidal or self-harming thoughts increases the overall risk of suicide. While standardized assessment measures cannot substitute for an in-person assessment, several assessment measures – including the Index of Depressive Symptomatology (IDS), the Hamilton Depression Rating Scale (HDRS), and the Beck Depression Inventory (BDI-II) – have items that specifically assess for suicidality and hopelessness. An additional measure, the Beck Hopelessness Scale, a 20-question self-report inventory, assesses the patient's hopelessness and negative beliefs about the future, both risk factors for suicide (Beck, Weissman, & Lester, 1974).

Assessment of demographic and environmental factors

The clinician will also want to carefully assess the following areas: history of psychiatric disorders, especially mood disorders, including substance abuse, history of suicidal behaviors, early family history (especially presence of physical or sexual abuse), specific family history of suicidal behavior, current or immediate psychosocial stressors, psychosocial supports, and coping skills and assets.

For patients with bipolar disorder, the illness itself is likely to contribute to the presence of a number of psychosocial stressors, including interpersonal losses, financial difficulties, changes in socioeconomic status, family conflict, and employment-related problems.

The clinician will want to assess for individual strengths and assets such as: the presence of good coping skills that might be adaptive in dealing with stress, engagement in treatment, medication adherence, the presence of a good therapeutic relationship, and the ability to tolerate psychological pain and distress.

There are several studies that examined suicide risk factors for patients diagnosed with bipolar disorder, including a review of a large sample of patients with bipolar disorder (Leverich et al., 2003) and a review on suicidal behavior in bipolar disorder (Tondo, Isacsson, & Baldessarini, 2003).

Management of Suicide Risk

Management of suicide risk

A general principle for managing suicide risk is that patients with suicidal thoughts, plans, or behaviors should be treated in the least restrictive setting that is safe and effective. The clinician should consider a broad range of interventions that might be instituted for patients with suicidal thoughts, plans, or behaviors. The range of possible treatment options to be considered includes: changing frequency and intensity of sessions; involving immediate family

Table of risk factors specific to bipolar disorder

Table 37
Suicide Risk Factors Specific to Bipolar Disorder (summarized from Leverich et al., 2003; Tondo et al., 2003)

- Severity of current depressive episode
- Previous episodes of severe depression
- Total number of hospitalizations
- Dysphoric agitated states
- Hopelessness
- Early childhood physical or sexual abuse
- Bipolar II disorder subtype

members or significant others; providing scheduled telephone follow-ups to monitor the patient between sessions, consulting with colleagues (highly recommended); referring patient for immediate psychiatric assessment; consulting with the treating psychiatrist; or recommending a more restrictive setting, including partial hospital, intensive outpatient, residential, or inpatient treatment; and/or instituting an immediate involuntary hospitalization. The *APA Guidelines* suggest that a hospital admission after a suicide attempt is generally indicated if the patient is psychotic, has had a significant change in mental status, has persistent suicidal ideation, is distressed or regrets surviving, is impulsive, severely agitated, demonstrates poor judgment; or if the attempt was violent, near lethal, or premeditated and the patient has limited psychosocial supports.

Bongar, Berman, Maris, Harris, and Packman (1992) summarize good risk management strategies for the clinician when working with suicidal patients in general as follows:

- Make every effort to identify factors that would indicate an elevated risk of suicide.
- Make every effort to reduce or eliminate this risk.
- In both initial assessment and ongoing clinical work, document management of risk in detail.
- Routinely consider a second opinion.

Summary of suicide risk management principles

4.5.2   Improving Treatment Adherence

This section addresses the critical importance of treatment adherence. Noncompliance with prescribed medication is a significant problem for patients with bipolar disorder, according to a number of estimates running as high as 40 50%. Nonadherence poses significant additional risks, including an increased risk of suicide, hospitalization, and the potentially devastating social and financial consequences associated with an acute manic or depressed episode. Several strategies have emerged that appear to be particularly useful in increasing medication adherence in this population. While the causes of nonadherence are complex and multidetermined, it is assumed that a collaborative treatment partnership in which the patient feels empowered to actively discuss treatment options and side effects will enhance treatment adherence. Conversely, an authoritarian "Doctor knows best" approach is likely to undermine adherence. Effective interventions may utilize a number of strategies to optimize adherence, including psychoeducation, emphasis on active collaboration, use of thought records to target unhelpful or dysfunctional assumptions about medication, and a motivational interviewing approach to help patients evaluate the costs and benefits of their decision-making process on medication and treatment options.

Improving treatment adherence

Addressing Issues Related to Session Attendance and Drop-Out

Addressing drop-out

In Section 4.1.4: Initial Phase of Treatment: Orientation and Engagement, we addressed a number of issues related to strategies to enhance treatment engagement and motivation. Certain individuals, typically more unstable or lower functioning patients seen in community mental health clinic settings, may experience significant attendance problems, motivational problems, and difficulty following through on assigned tasks. This is especially true for individuals with bipolar disorder who have inherent, biologically based difficulties with self-regulation, maintaining structure and routines, and completing assigned tasks. It is also true of depressed demoralized patients who feel hopeless and have trouble consistently viewing treatment as necessary and useful. In order to address initial problems with attendance and attrition, the clinician will want to supplement standard treatment with weekly and periodic extratreatment patient contacts in order to enhance engagement in treatment and adherence. Patients should receive reminder calls in the 24 hours before scheduled group or individual sessions. Patients who miss sessions should routinely receive follow-up calls and homework assignments over the telephone. Patients who miss two or more consecutive treatment session or identified as at high risk for drop should receive calls directly from the practitioner or group facilitators. In some cases, calls may be made by office assistants or other clinic personnel, including case managers.

Helping Patients Follow Through on Homework Assignments

Addressing homework compliance

Patients may have difficulty completing homework assignments, and this may be linked directly to problems with attendance and dropping out of treatment altogether. In our experience, patients often need in-session coaching in order to successfully complete their homework assignments – a key requirement for a skills-based treatment model that requires active participation. Patients may avoid coming to sessions because they feel guilty or inadequate for failing to complete homework assignments. When assigning homework it is always important to address any potential problems and barriers that the patient anticipates. Patients often worry that the therapist will be angry with them for not following through or having problems completing homework. In a previous section we also addressed the potential impact of feelings of hopelessness and

Demoralization as a factor in non-compliance

demoralization as barriers to completing therapy tasks. If the patient appears to have any specific emotional reactions, these should be addressed directly with the patient when making assignments. It is often useful to determine the patient's level of confidence that they will be able to complete their assignments ("How confident are you that you will be able to complete this assignment on a scale of 0–100?"). If confidence is low, it is wise to scale back the complexity of the task until a level of higher confidence is reached. Often a problem-solving approach is most fruitful in increasing adherence to this aspect of treatment.

Addressing Problems with Medication Adherence

Addressing medication compliance: behavioral tailoring strategies

In dealing with medication adherence, a primary problem for patients with bipolar disorder, follow a hierarchy of problem-solving strategies, starting with the most simple, pragmatic solutions. Research supports the value of assisting the patient in developing specific, concrete strategies to improve medication adherence (Mueser et al., 2002). Meichenbaum and Turk (1987, Table 21, p. 140) review interventions designed to help the patient remember to take their medication.

A general principle is to start by addressing the problem at the simplest level first, and then proceed hierarchically to more complex solutions. For example, if a behavioral tailoring approach does not appear to be addressing the underlying issues, then we recommend proceeding to an analysis of the patient's beliefs about medication and her or his illness to identify unhelpful beliefs that are compromising adherence. There are complex and multiple determinants associated with nonadherence. Table 40 summarizes key points from Meichenbaum and Turk (1987) associated with beliefs regarding illness and medication that may compromise adherence.

Table 38
Behavioral Tailoring (adapted from Meichenbaum & Turk, 1987)

- Involve family members when appropriate
- Alarms, small pocket timers, or use of PDAs with alarm
- Drug reminder charts
- Yellow "Post-Its" on the medicine cabinet or refrigerator
- Special calendars (available from the Depression and Bipolar Support Alliance)
- Medication boxes – separated by day and by time of dose
- Special pill boxes with time alarm reminders
- Medication strategically placed and coordinated with daily routine (e.g., bathroom sink, breakfast table)
- Call patient to remind

Table 39
Reasons for Non-Adherence (adapted from Meichenbaum & Turk, 1987)

- Uncertainty about the effectiveness of treatment
- Expectations about the course of illness
- Past experiences in treatment
- Concerns about side effects
- Determination that costs outweigh potential benefits
- Stigma associated with psychiatric medication
- Sense of hopelessness or fatalism
- Conflicts with cultural or family belief systems

Reasons for non-adherence

A review of the literature on bipolar disorder tells us that almost 50% of patients are likely to have problems with medication adherence. In our experience it is rarely useful to become directive, confrontational, or irritated with patients who have adherence problems. As an alternative to more directive approaches, motivational interviewing (MI) provides a noncoercive strategy that supports the patient's concerns and issues. The goal of MI is to avoid the trap of becoming directive and attempting to get patients to "comply" (e.g., give in), thereby damaging the therapeutic alliance and increasing conflict. MI attempts to engage the patient in a self-directed discussion of the pros and cons of medication adherence, with a focus on getting the patient to recognize how nonadherence is ultimately inconsistent with other specified goals and values and may have negative consequences that they do not wish to experience.

Clinical dialogue:
Addressing
medication
compliance:
behavioral tailoring
strategies

Clinical Vignette

Behavioral Tailoring for Medication Adherence

Therapist: Are there any other problems that we want to make sure we address?

Patient: Yes. One consistent problem for me has been keeping up with actually taking my medication. When I'm at home I'm fine, but then back at school I stop taking it after about a month. I don't know why.

Therapist: Do you say to yourself that I'm going to stop, or do you just find yourself not remembering?

Patient: I forget OK. I can't figure out what's going on

Therapist: And what's the difference between home and school in terms of taking your medication?

Patient: I guess I kind of planted in my head the idea that if Mom asks me I need to say "Yes".

Therapist: Do you depend on reminders from other people?

Patient: I guess it's a kind of mental trick that I had better take it in case Mom asks – she knows I have had trouble at school.

Therapist: So, when no one asks you, that's when you run into trouble?

Patient: es. I really don't have any idea why or how that ends up happening, it just happens.

Therapist: So you don't seem to be doing on purpose, you just seem to lapse suddenly.

Patient: Yes, suddenly I've been off my medications weeks and feeling horribly depressed and not attending classes. I'm a wreck.

Therapist: So its sounds important that this not happen again. It seems like when you're at home you have a cueing system that eventually comes in and says, "Oh, by the way, did you take your medicine?" and you're using that to cue yourself –problem is you don't have that same cueing system in college.

Patient: What I could do is use a calendar and make a specific mark each day signifying I took the pills.

Therapist: Ok, so you could mark your calendar. That's a good suggestion because then when you check your calendar you'll know where you stand, particularly if you're checking your calendar all the time anyway for other things you've scheduled. Maybe we could assign this as homework over the next week for you to keep a daily calendar on medication. I think I warned you I might give homework.

Patient: Well, it's my idea anyway – so this assignment is my fault!

Therapist: So you accept responsibility for this one, since you developed yourself.

Addressing Unhelpful Beliefs about Medication

Addressing unhelpful
beliefs about
medication

A powerful strategy of addressing medication nonadherence after initiating more detail-oriented efforts in terms of medication tailoring and communication issues can be addressing the patient's unhelpful beliefs about medication and stigmatizing beliefs about their illness directly, through an "Unhelpful Thought Record." Problems with medication adherence are often tied up with stigmatizing and unhelpful thoughts about the meaning of having a chronic illness and taking a psychiatric medication. It is useful to use an analogy of patients with diabetes who are faced with managing a long-term illness through a variety of strategies, including changes in behavior (eating and exercise), careful monitoring of blood sugar levels, and consistent use of medication to manage their illness.

Patients can be asked directly what thoughts they had prior to making a decision to stop taking their medication. In some cases, patients will indicate that they no longer "feel ill" and believe that the medication is no longer required. One of our patients reported that, "I knew I wasn't ill any longer when my thoughts became clearer and so I stopped taking my medication." In this case, the sense experienced by the patient of clarity in their thinking was actually associated with a hypomanic episode. The therapist developed a strategy in which this sense of new clarity was actually interpreted as a warning sign, indicating that it was time for the patient to monitor closely and take action in terms of instituting a coping plan. Often patients will articulate a number of catastrophic beliefs about bipolar disorder which results in feelings of pessimism and hopelessness. Patients can also experience "dependence" on medication as threatening to their sense of autonomy. This can be reframed as "taking control over the illness" by managing their health proactively.

4.5.3 Treatment of Patients with Co-Occurring Substance Use Disorders

It is widely recognized that a high percentage of patients with bipolar disorder also present with a history of substance use disorders. Patients may use substances in an attempt to either counteract specific symptoms of depression (e.g., insomnia, depressed mood, lethargy) and hypomania/mania (agitation, anxiety) or to prolong hypomanic episodes. In a large national trial, the STEP-BD program, 20% of eligible subjects with a bipolar I or bipolar II diagnosis were also diagnosed with a current substance use disorder. Other estimates of co-occurring substance use disorders range from 40% 60% lifetime prevalence (Baldessarini, 2002; Biederman, Faraone, Wozniak, & Monuteaux, 2000; Dalton, Cate Carter, Mundo, Parikh, & Kennedy, 2003; Zarate & Tohen, 2001). Because the use of substances significantly impacts the course of the illness, as well as medication and treatment adherence, optimal treatment of the co-occurring disorder requires concurrent treatment of both disorders. The intervention incorporates the use of a motivational interviewing approach first developed by Miller and Rollnick (2002) to assist patients in evaluating the impact of their substance use.

Treating co-occurring substance use disorders

Addressing Comorbid Substance Use with Motivational Interviewing Strategies

As noted above, comorbid substance abuse is a significant risk factor. Based on the data reviewed earlier it is important to assume that your patients are misusing drugs until you rule out this possibility. It is important to address substance misuse in the context of why the patient is misusing substances in terms of coping with stress, depression, or attempting to avoid certain negative affects, interpersonal conflicts, or other problems.

Clinical Vignette
The Case of Bob – "Using Marijuana to Fit In"

Bob is a 35-year-old sculptor whose primary support group comprises primarily artists and their friends. The topic of comorbid substance abuse came up in a group meeting that triggered the following conversation:

Clinical dialogue: Using motivational interviewing strategies to address substance misuse

Bob:	My problem is that I hang out with this group of artists who smoke marijuana. I feel like I need to smoke with them to keep my social bonding. It's insidious, because it reduces my depression but it makes me psychotic.
Therapist:	Can we look at this for a moment Bob, and maybe to see what are some of the harmful things that might occur as a result of your smoking marijuana, and maybe what you see as some of the benefits?
Bob:	It's my psychotic paranoia that bothers me most.
Therapist:	We're almost out of time, and it seems that it might be a good idea to make a little list of the pros and cons of smoking marijuana for you.
Bob:	Yeah.
Therapist:	Do you think that next time you could bring in a list of pros and cons? Maybe we could discuss it with the group, since you brought it up. We could look at balancing the two. Would you be willing to go over this at the next session.
Bob:	Yeah. I can do that.

Following week at check in when it was Bob's turn to report about his week:

Therapist:	Bob, were you able to make the list as you had planned?
Bob:	Yeah.
Therapist:	For the benefit of those who weren't here last time, we got into the issue of marijuana use, and as we talked about it, we asked Bob if he would be willing to list some of the pros and cons of his marijuana use.
Bob:	Well I haven't had any for the last few weeks except some that Gail brought over last Saturday night. We smoked it together and it wasn't so good. When I get into the benefits and costs of using, the benefits are that it lifted feelings of depression temporarily. It also lifted feelings of anger temporarily. Of feeling overwhelmed. And it apparently helped with social bonding with the group, in having a shared experience. The problems were that it increased the paranoia, it increased the psychotic feelings.
Therapist:	You mentioned psychotic feelings. What does that mean to you?
Bob:	You mean the paranoia?
Therapist:	Well, and the psychotic feelings.
Bob:	Well I'm not sure how to say it. The paranoia would be included also, but uh, uh, uh, I'm not sure how to describe it. It's feeling different; like not knowing where self ends and the rest of the world begins. I don't mean that its unpleasant. It's actually a little pleasant, but can't function. Then when I'm home and lonely, I smoke it to make myself feel better, which leads to paranoia, which leads to being even more lonely, and then I smoke more. So it's kind of a vicious cycle.
Therapist:	So you get some short tem relief that is a positive effect, but a more long-term consequence is that it increases loneliness and depression
Bob:	Right, so then I wrote this thing that I don't want to give up social bonding. It's important to have a peer group, so I thought maybe I should just smoke it in the group and never take it home with me, but then after this Saturday, I realized that I had this paranoia even when smoking with someone else. So there really are not any benefits.

Therapist:	You were hoping that this would make you closer to the group, but as you look at it you're not sure ...?
Bob:	Yeah, I do it for social bonding, but then wonder if I'm being appropriate and I get paranoid, and then I want to get away from the group, so that's not working as I thought. So the only thing left as an explanation is that the whole group is playing monopoly and I'm not playing.
Therapist:	Seems like the social bonding is the important thing here, maybe the group has ideas about ways of bonding that are not harmful. Is that where you're stuck?
Bob:	Yeah, I really want to have the bonding.
Therapist:	Are you accepted by the group or do you have to smoke to be in the group?
Bob:	Well, that's a real problem. I don't know. I feel they do accept me as an artist, but then there is this other aspect that I can't just calculate.
Group Member:	Can you come up with substitute like a double latte?
Bob:	I should probably let it be known that they should not offer it to me.
Therapist:	How would you feel if you said to them "I don't want to do this"?
Bob:	I think it would be okay. I don't think they would get rid of me. I think if I said I still want to be in the group, but I just don't want to smoke the stuff because of the way it makes me feel, that this would be OK.
Therapist:	Are you ready to do that as an experiment?
Bob:	Yeah, I don't want to give them up. It helped a lot to write this down.
Therapist:	Do you think you can say this to them?
Bob:	Yeah.
Therapist:	Would it help if we did a role play?
Bob:	No, that's OK. I'll be able to tell them. Though, it's scary when you have to give something like that up. I'll try it with them and then report back. If I can stand a little outside the circle it'll be better. Thank you for going over this with me. This was helpful.

Eight months later during feedback at last booster session of the group:

Bob:	One of the good things about this group is that it helped me stop smoking marijuana. No one here yelled at me or anything that I had to stop using dope. I would probably have just ignored that. But you helped me look at what I thought I was getting out of smoking and what it was really doing to me, and I was able to make my own decision to stop.

Clinical Vignette

Assessing the Cost and Benefits of Substance Misuse

Clinical dialogue: Determining the costs and benefits of substance misuse

Therapist:	So, we talked about a possible look at the pros and cons of alcohol and drug use for you. Would you be interested in exploring this further?
Patient:	Well, I usually smoke pot when I'm feeling bored and then I watch TV.
Therapist:	OK, [going to board to write down exercise] so here's a way of looking at the benefits and costs of any thing your doing. So you have told me one of the benefits of smoking pot is that it prevents you from being bored, is that right?

Patient:	Yeah, I can smoke pot all day and watch TV and never get bored.
Therapist:	[joking] Well, that's strong drug – one that makes TV interesting. I ll put down "makes TV interesting" as a benefit.
Patient:	[laughing] OK
Therapist:	Do you sometime smoke pot when your feeling stressed or depressed?
Patient:	Yeah, it relives my depression. It makes my problems seem trivial.
Therapist:	What are some of the other benefits?
Patient:	There really is none. It makes me less social.
Therapist:	So I'll put that under "Costs".
Patient:	'Cause I don't carry on a conversation very well and it's hard to concentrate.
Therapist:	Well, you also mentioned you have to pass a drug test, so you can't apply for a new job which you'd like to do. Is that a cost too?
Patient:	Yeah. Also sometimes I sleep a lot. Also I'll drink 10 beers a night.
Therapist:	Is that a problem for you?
Patient:	Well, I sleep a lot and feel hung over about once a week.
Therapist:	Does alcohol improve your mood or give you relief from anxiety?
Therapist:	Have we covered everything on our list?
Patient:	Well, marijuana makes me lazy
Therapist:	Is that a problem?
Patient:	Not really.
Therapist:	Is our list complete in terms of the benefits and costs? You've talked about a long-term goal of meeting a woman also – how does this get affected by your marijuana and alcohol use.
Patient:	If I quit alcohol it'll be a roller coaster.
Therapist:	So, that will be a cost?
Patient:	Yes.

4.6   Summary

Clinicians working with patients with bipolar disorder are likely to confront a number of specific clinical challenges, including suicide risk, problems with treatment adherence, and comorbid substance use disorders. A number of specific strategies that target each of these problems have been outlined above. In order to be successful, clinicians need to be willing to be flexible in their treatment approach and to incorporate a number of specialized interventions into a more standardized evidence-based treatment approach.

5

Further Reading

This section includes key references to literature where the practitioner can find further details or background information. Each reference includes a brief (2–5 lines) annotation.

Basco, M.R., & Rush, A. John (1996). *Cognitive-behavioral therapy for Bipolar Disorder.* New York: Guilford. The earliest comprehensive psychosocial treatment manual for bipolar disorder focusing on cognitive and behavioral strategies with many specific and useful tools for the practitioner.

Bauer, M., & McBride, L. (2003). *Structured group therapy for bipolar disorder: the life goals program.* New York: Springer Publishing Company. The only group-based treatment approach with a full length treatment manual.

Beck, A.T., Rush, A.J., Shaw, B.F., & Emery, G. (1979). *Cognitive therapy of depression.* New York: Guilford. An excellent teaching manual and reference for basic techniques of cognitive-behavior therapy. Despite its "age," it remains a primary source for techniques of cognitive therapy.

Beck, J. (1995). *Cognitive Therapy: Basics and Beyond.* New York: Guilford. An excellent teaching manual and reference for basic techniques of cognitive-behavior therapy.

Goodwin, F. K., & Jamison, K. R. (1990). *Manic-depressive illness.* New York: Oxford University Press. A comprehensive research based resource textbook addressing many aspects of bipolar disorder – still the best overall summary available.

Lam, D. H., Jones, S. H., Hayward, P., & Bright, J. A. (1999). *Cognitive therapy for bipolar disorder: a therapist's guide to concepts, methods and practice.* New York: John Wiley. The first cognitive-behavioral treatment manual for bipolar disorder to comprehensively address the role of early intervention with prodromal symptoms.

Miklowitz, D.J., & Goldstein, M.J. (1997). *Bipolar disorder: a family-focused approach.* New York: Guilford. The first comprehensive evidence-based treatment manual addressing a family-based approach with bipolar disorder.

Miklowitz, D.J. (2002). *The bipolar disorder survival guide: what you and your family need to know.* New York: Guilford. An excellent resource for clients with bipolar disorder and family members. This popular book is clearly written and well researched and includes specific coping tools and other resources that are highly valuable.

Newman, C.F., Leahy, R.L., Beck, A.T., Reilly-Harrington, N.A., & Gyulai, L. (2002). *Bipolar disorder: a cognitive therapy approach.* Washington, DC: American Psychological Association. An excellent summary of cognitive strategies with bipolar disorder.

Persons, J., Davidson, J., & Tompkins, M.A. (2001). *Essential components of cognitive behavioral therapy for depression.* Washington, DC: American Psychological Association. An excellent teaching manual and reference for basic techniques of cognitive-behavior therapy.

Scott, J. (2001). *Overcoming mood swings: a self-help guide to using cognitive behavioral techniques.* New York: New York University Press. An excellent self-help guide incorporating key cognitive behavioral strategies for patients with bipolar disorder.

6

References

Akiskal, H.S. (2005). Mood disorders: Clinical features. In B.J. Sadock & V.A. Sadock (Eds.), *Kaplan & Sadock's comprehensive textbook of psychiatry* (8th ed., Vol. I, pp. 1611–1652). Philadelphia: Lippincott, Williams & Wilkins.

Altman, E.G., Hedeker, D.R., Peterson, J.L., & Davis, J.M. (1997). The Altman Self-Rating Mania Scale. *Biological Psychiatry, 42,* 948–955.

American Psychiatric Association (2000). *Diagnostic and statistical manual of mental disorders: DSM-IV-TR* (4th ed.). Washington, DC: APA.

American Psychiatric Association. (2004). *Practice guidelines for the treatment of psychiatric disorders*. Arlington, VA: APA.

Angst, J., Sellaro, R., & Angst, F. (1998). Long-term outcome and mortality of treated versus untreated bipolar and depressed patients: A preliminary report. *International Journal of Psychiatry in Clinical Practice, 2*(2), 115–119.

Baldessarini, R.J. (2002). Treatment research in bipolar disorder: issues and recommendations. *CNS Drugs, 16*(11), 721–729.

Barlow, D.H. (2001). *Clinical handbook of psychological disorders: a step-by-step treatment manual* (3rd ed.). New York: Guilford Press.

Basco, M.R., & Rush, A.J. (1996). *Cognitive-behavioral therapy for bipolar disorder*. New York: Guilford Press.

Beck, A.T., & Garbin, M.G. (1988). Psychometric properties of the Beck Depression Inventory: Twenty-five years of evaluation. *Clinical Psychology Review, 8*(1), 77–100.

Beck, A.T., Rush, A.J., Shaw, B.F., & Emery, G. (1979). *Cognitive therapy of depression*. New York: Guilford Press.

Beck, A.T., Weissman, A., & Lester, D. (1974). The measurement of pessimism: The Hopelessness Scale. *Journal of Consulting & Clinical Psychology, 42*(6), 861–865.

Benazzi, F., & Akiskal, H. (2003). Clinical and factor-analytic validation of depressive mixed states: A report from the Ravenna-San Diego collaboration. *Current Opinion in Psychiatry, 16* (Suppl 2), S71–S78.

Biederman, J., Faraone, S.V., Wozniak, J., & Monuteaux, M.C. (2000). Parsing the association between bipolar, conduct, and substance use disorders: A familial risk analysis. *Biological Psychiatry, 48*(11), 1037–1044.

Blanch, A., Fisher, D., Tucker, W., & Chassmann, J. (1997). Consumer-practioners share insights about recovery and coping. In L. Spaniol, M. Koehler, & C. Gagne (Eds.), *Psychological and social aspects of psychiatric disability*. Boston: Boston University Center for Psychiatric Rehabilitation.

Bongar, B., Berman, A., Maris, R.W., Harris, E., Packman, W.L. (1992). *Risk management with suicidal patients*. New York: Guilford Press.

Burns, D. (1999). *Feeling good: The new mood therapy*. New York: Avon Books.

Cochran, S.D. (1984). Preventing medication non-compliance in the outpatient treatment of bipolar affective disorders. *Journal of Consulting and Clinical Psychology, 52*(5) 873–878.

Colom, F., Vieta, E., & Martinez-Arán, A. (2003). A randomized trial on the efficacy of group psychoeducation in the prophylaxis of recurrences in bipolar patients whose disease is in remission. *Archives of General Psychiatry, 60*(4), 402–407.

Dalton, E.J., Cate Carter, T.D., Mundo, E., Parikh, S.V., & Kennedy, J.L. (2003). Suicide risk in bipolar patients: The role of co-morbid substance use disorders. *Bipolar Disorders, 5*(1), 58–61.

Denticoff, K.D., Leverich, G.S., Nolen, W.A., Rush, A.J., McElroy, S.L., Keck, P.E., & Suppes, X.Y. (2000). Validation of the prospective NIMH-Life-Chart Method (NIMH-LCM-super (TM)-p) for longitudinal assessment of bipolar illness. *Psychological Medicine, 30*(6), 1391–1397.

Dixon, L., McFarlane, W.R., & Lefley, H. (2001). Evidence-based practices for services to families of people with psychiatric disabilities. *Psychiatric Services, 52*(7), 903–910.

Ehlers, C.L., Frank, E., & Kupfer, D.J. (1988). Social zeitgebers and biological rhythms. *Archives of General Psychiatry, 45*(10), 948–952.

Frank, E., Hlastala, S., Ritenour, A., Houck, P., Tu, X.M., Monk, T.H., et al. (1997). Inducing lifestyle regularity in recovering bipolar disorder patients: Results from the maintenance therapies in bipolar disorder protocol. *Biological Psychiatry, 41*(12), 1165–1173.

Frank, E., Swartz, H.A., & Kupfer, D.J. (2000). Interpersonal and social rhythm therapy: Managing the chaos of bipolar disorder. *Biological Psychiatry, 48*(6), 593–604.

Frank, E., Swartz, H.A., Mallinger, A.G., Thase, M.E., Weaver, E.V., & Kupfer, D.J. (1999). Adjunctive psychotherapy for bipolar disorder: Effects of changing treatment modality. *Journal of Abnormal Psychology, 108*(4), 579–587.

Goldstein, M.J., & Miklowitz, D.J. (1994). Family intervention for persons with bipolar disorder. *New Directions in Mental Health Services, 62*, 23–35.

Goodwin, F.K., & Jamison, K.R. (1990). *Manic-depressive illness*. New York: Oxford University Press.

Greenhouse, W.J., Meyer, B., & Johnson, S.L. (2000). Coping and medication adherence in bipolar disorder. *Journal of Affective Disorders, 59*(3), 237–241.

Gutierrez, M.J., & Scott, J. (2004). Psychological treatment for bipolar disorders: A review of randomized controlled trials. *European Archives of Psychiatry and Clinical Neuroscience, 254*(2), 92–99.

Harrington, R., & Myatt, T. (2003). Is preadolescent mania the same condition as adult mania? A British perspective. *Biological Psychiatry, 53*(11), 961–969.

Hirschfeld, D.R., Gould, R.A., Reilly-Harrington, N.A., Morabito, C., Cosgrove, V., Guille, V., Friedman, S., & Sachs, G.S. (1998). Short-term adjunctive cognitive-behavioral group therapy for bipolar disorder: Preliminary results from a controlled trial. Paper presented at a meeting of the Association for the Advancement of Behavior Therapy, Washington, DC.

Hirschfeld, R.M., Williams, J.B., Spitzer, R.L., Calabrese, J.R., Flynn, L., Keck, P.E., Jr., et al. (2000). Development and validation of a screening instrument for bipolar spectrum disorder: The Mood Disorder Questionnaire. *American Journal of Psychiatry, 157*(11), 1873–1875.

Hilty, D.M., Brady, K.T., & Hales, R.E. (1999). A review of bipolar disorder among adults. *Psychiatric Services, 50*(2), 201–213.

Huxley, N.A., Parikh, S.V., & Baldessarini, R.J. (2000). Effectiveness of psychosocial treatments in bipolar disorder: State of the evidence. *Harvard Review of Psychiatry, 8*(3), 126–140.

International Consensus Group on Bipolar I Depression Guidelines. (2004). *Journal of Clinical Psychiatry, 65*(4), 569–579.

Johnson, S.L., & Leahy, R.L. (2004). *Psychological treatment of bipolar disorder*. New York: Guilford Press.

Judd, L.L., Akiskal, H.S., Schettler, P.J., Coryell, W., Maser, J., Rice, J.A., et al. (2003). The comparative clinical phenotype and long term longitudinal episode course of bipolar I and II: A clinical spectrum or distinct disorders? *Journal of Affective Disorders, 73*(1), 1932.

Kent, L., & Craddock, N. (2003). Is there a relationship between attention deficit hyperactivity disorder and bipolar disorder? *Journal of Affective Disorders, 73*(3), 211–221.

Kessler, R.C. (1999). "Patterns and predictors of treatment contact after first onset of psychiatric disorders": Reply. *American Journal of Psychiatry, 156*(5), 812.

Kessler, R.C., Borges, G. & Walters, E.E. (1999). Prevalence of and risk factors for lifetime suicide attempts in the National Comorbidity Survey. *Archives of General Psychiatry, 56*(7), 617–626.

Lam, D., & Gale, J. (2000). Cognitive behavior therapy: Teaching a client the ABC model – the first step towards the process of change. *Journal of Advanced Nursing, 31*(2), 444–451.

Lam, D., & Wong, G. (1997). Prodromes, coping strategies, insight and social functioning in bipolar affective disorders. *Psychological Medicine, 27*(5), 1091–1100.

Lam, D., Wong, G., & Sham, P. (2001). Prodromes, coping strategies and course of illness in bipolar affective disorder – a naturalistic study. *Psychological Medicine, 31*(8), 1397–1402.

Lam, D.H., Bright, J., Jones, S., Hayward, P., Schuck, N., Chisholm, D., & Sham, P. (2000). Cognitive therapy for bipolar illness: A pilot study of relapse prevention. *Cognitive Therapy & Research, 24*(50), 503–521.

Lam, D.H., Hayward, P., Watkins, E.R., Wright, K., & Sham, P. (2005). Relapse prevention in patients with bipolar disorder: Cognitive therapy outcome after 2 years. *American Journal of Psychiatry, 162*(2), 324–329.

Lam, D.H., Jones, S.H., Hayward, P., & Bright, J. (1999). *Cognitive therapy for bipolar disorder: A therapist's guide to concepts, methods, and practice.* Chichester, NY: Wiley.

Lam, D.H., Watkins, E.R., Hayward, P., Bright, J., Wright, K., Kerr, N., et al. (2003). A randomized controlled study of cognitive therapy for relapse prevention for bipolar affective disorder: Outcome of the first year. *Archives of General Psychiatry, 60*(2), 145–152.

Lambert, M.J. (2004). *Bergin and Garfield's handbook of psychotherapy and behavior change* (5th ed.). New York: Wiley.

Leverich, G.S., Altshuler, L.L., & Frye, M.A. (2003). Factors associated with suicide attempts in 648 patients with bipolar disorder in the Stanley Foundation Bipolar Network. *Journal of Clinical Psychiatry, 64*(5), 506–515.

Lewinsohn, P.M., Munoz, R.F., Youngren, M.A., & Zeiss, A.M. (1986). *Control your depression.* New York: Prentice Hall.

Maier, W., & Sandmann, J. (1993). Validation of diagnoses according to psychiatric diagnostic manuals in follow-up studies, exemplified by affective and schizophrenic diseases. *Nervenarzt, 64*(3), 160–168.

Malkoff-Schwartz, S., Frank, E., & Anderson, B. (1998). Stressful life events and social rhythm disruption in the onset of manic and depressive bipolar episodes. *Archives of General Psychiatry, 55*(8), 702–707.

Marlatt, G.A. (1996). Models of relapse and relapse prevention: A commentary. *Journal of Experimental and Clinical Psychopharmacology, 4*, 55–60.

McIntyre, R.S., Konarski, J.Z., & Yatham, L.N. (2004). Comorbidity in bipolar disorder: A framework for rational treatment selection. *Human Psychopharmacology, 19*(6), 369–386.

Meichenbaum, D., & Turk, D.C. (1987). *Facilitating treatment adherence: A practitioner's guide.* New York: Plenum Press.

Merikangas, K.R., & Low N.C.P. (2004). The epidemiology of mood disorders. *Current Psychiatry Reports, 6*, 411–421.

Miklowitz, D.J. (2002). *The bipolar disorder survival guide: What you and your family need to know.* New York: Guilford Press.

Miklowitz, D.J. (2004). The role of family systems in severe and recurrent psychiatric disorders: A developmental psychopathology view. *Developmental Psychopathology, 16*(3), 667–688.

Miklowitz, D.J., & Alloy, L.B. (1999). Psychosocial factors in the course and treatment of bipolar disorder: Introduction to the special section. *Journal of Abnormal Psychology, 108*(4), 555–557.

Miklowitz, D.J., George, E.L., Richards, J.A., Simoneau, T.L., & Suddath, R.L. (2003). A randomized study of family-focused psychoeducation and pharmacotherapy in the outpatient management of bipolar disorder. *Archives of General Psychiatry, 60*(9), 904–912.

Miklowitz, D.J., & Goldstein, M.J. (1997). *Bipolar disorder: A family-focused treatment.* New York: Guilford Press.

Miklowitz, D.J., Goldstein, M.J., Nuechterlein, K.H., Snyder, K.S., & Mintz, J. (1988). Family factors and the course of bipolar affective disorder. *Archives of General Psychiatry, 45*(3), 225–231.

Miller, W.R., & Rollnick, S. (2002). *Motivational interviewing: Preparing people for change* (2nd ed.). New York: Guilford Press.

Mueser, K.T., Corrigan, P.W., Hilton, D.W., Tanzman, B., Schaub, A., Gingerich, S., et al. (2002). Illness management and recovery: A review of the research. *Psychiatric Services, 53*(10), 1272–1284.

Newman, C.F., Leahy, R.L., Beck, A.T., Reilly-Harrington, N., & Gyulai, L. (2002). *Bipolar disorder: A cognitive therapy approach.* Washington, DC: American Psychological Association.

Peele, P.B., Xu, Y., & Kupfer, D.J. (2003). Insurance expenditures on bipolar disorder: Clinical and parity implications. *American Journal of Psychiatry, 160*(7), 1286–1290.

Perry, A., Tarrier, N., Morriss, R., McCarthy, E., & Limb, K. (1999). Randomised controlled trial of efficacy of teaching patients with bipolar disorder to identify early symptoms of relapse and obtain treatment. *British Medical Journal, 318*(7177), 149–153.

Post, R.M., & Altshuler, L.L. (2005). Mood disorders: Treatment of bipolar disorders. In B.J. Sadock & V.A. Sadock (Eds.), *Kaplan & Sadock's comprehensive textbook of psychiatry* (8th ed.). Philadelphia: Lippincott, Williams & Wilkins.

Post, R.M., & Leverich, G.S. (1997). *The NIMH life chart manual for recurrent affective illness.* Bethesda, MD: National Institute of Mental Health.

Post, R.M., Leverich, G.S., Altshuler, L.L., Frye, M.A., Suppes, T., Keck, P.E., et al. (2003). An overview of recent findings of the Stanley Foundation bipolar network (Part I). *Bipolar Disorders, 5*, 310–319.

Post, R.M., Roy-Byrne, P.P., & Uhde, T.W. (1988). Graphic representation of the life course of illness in patients with affective disorder. *Archives of General Psychiatry, 145*(7), 844–848.

Rihmer, Z., & Angst, J. (2005). Mood disorders: Epidemiology. In B.J. Sadock & V.A. Sadock (Eds.), *Kaplan & Sadock's comprehensive textbook of psychiatry* (8th ed., Vol. I, pp. 1575–1582). Philadelphia: Lippincott, Williams & Wilkins.

Rush, A.J., Giles, D.E., & Schlesser, M.A. (1985). The Inventory of Depressive Symptomatology (IDS): Preliminary findings. *Psychiatric Resources, 18*, 65–87.

Rush, A.J., Gullion, B.B., & Basco, M.R. (1996). The Inventory of Depressive Symptomatology (IDS): Psychometric properties. *Psychological Medicine, 26*, 477–486.

Sachs, G.S. (2004). Strategies for improving treatment of bipolar disorder: integration of measurement and management. *Acta Psychiatrica Scandanavica, 110* (Suppl. 422), 7–17.

Sachs, G.S., & Cosgrove, V.E. (1998). Bipolar disorder: Current treatments and new strategies. *Cleveland Clinical Journal of Medicine, 65,* Suppl. 1, SI31–37; discussion SI45–37.

Sachs, G.S., Printz, D.J., Kahn D.A., Carpenter, D., & Doherty, J.P. (2000). The expert consensus guidelines series: Medication treatment for bipolar disorder. *Postgraduate Medicine,* April: 1–104.

Sadock, B.J., & Sadock, V.A. (Eds.). (2005) *Kaplan & Sadock's comprehensive textbook of psychiatry* (8th ed.). Philadelphia: Lippincott, Williams & Wilkins.

Scott, J. (2002). Using Health Belief Models to understand the efficacy-effectiveness gap for mood stabilizer treatments. *Neuropsychobiology, 46,* Suppl. 1, 13–15.

Scott, J., Garland, A., & Moorhead, S. (2001). A pilot study of cognitive therapy in bipolar disorders. *Psychological Medicine, 31*(3), 459–467.

Scott, J., & Pope, M. (2002). Self-reported adherence to treatment with mood stabilizers, plasma levels, and psychiatric hospitalization. *Archives of General Psychiatry, 159*(11), 1927–1929.

Scott, J., & Tacchi, M.J. (2002). A pilot study of concordance therapy for individuals with bipolar disorders who are non-adherent with lithium prophylaxis. *Bipolar Disorders, 4*(6), 386–392.

Serretti, A. (2002). Clinical and demographic features of mood disorder subtypes. *Psychiatry Research, 112*(3), 195–210.

Slama, F., Belliver, F., Henry, C., Rousseva, A., Etain, B., Rouillon, F., & Leboyer, M. (2004). Bipolar patients with suicidal behavior: Toward identification of a clinical subgroup. *Journal of Clinical Psychiatry, 65*, 1035–1039.

Spearing, M.K., Post, R.M., & Leverich, G.S. (1997). Modification of the Clinical Global Impressions (CGI) scale for use in bipolar illness (BP): The CGI-BP. *Psychiatry Research, 73*(3), 159–171.

Suppes, T., Swann, A.C., Dennehy, E.B., Habermacher, E.D., Mason, M., Crismon, M.L., et al. (2001). Texas Medication Algorithm Project: Development and feasibility testing of a treatment algorithm for patients with bipolar disorder. *Journal of Clinical Psychiatry, 62*(6), 439–447.

Tillman, R., Geller, B., Bolhofner, K., Craney, J.L., Williams, M., & Zimerman, B. (2003). Ages of onset and rates of syndromal and subsyndromal comorbid DSM-IV diagnoses in a prepubertal and early adolescent bipolar disorder phenotype. *Journal of the American Academy of Child and Adolescent Psychiatry, 42*(12), 1486–1493.

Tondo, L. Isacsson, G. & Baldessarini, R.J. (2003). Suicidal behaviour in bipolar disorder: Risk and prevention. *CNS Drugs, 17*(7), 491–512.

Thomas, P. (2004). The many forms of bipolar disorder: A modern look at an old illness. *Journal of Affective Disorders,79*, 3–8.

Williams, J.B.W. (1988). A structured interview guide for the Hamilton Depression Rating Scale. *Archives of General Psychiatry, 45*, 742–747.

Young, R.C., Biggs, J.T., & Ziegler, V.E. (1978). A rating scale for mania. *British Journal of Psychiatry, 133*, 429–435.

Zarate, C.A.J.R., & Tohen, M.F. (2001). Bipolar disorder and comorbid substance use disorders. In J.R. Hubbard & P.R. Martin (Eds.), *Substance abuse in the mentally and physically disabled* (pp. 59–75). New York: Marcel Dekker.

Zaretsky, A. (2003). Targeted psychosocial interventions for bipolar disorder. *Bipolar Disorders, 5,* Suppl. 2, 80–87.

7

Appendix: Tools and Resources

Comparison of DSM IV-TR and ICD-10 Diagnostic Coding

296.6x	Bipolar I Disorder, Most Recent Episode Mixed	F31.6	Bipolar affective disorder, current episode mixed
296.x5	In Partial Remission	F31.7	Bipolar affective
296.x6	In Full Remission		disorder, currently in remission
296.7	Bipolar I Disorder, Most Recent Episode Unspecified	F31.9	Bipolar affective disorder, unspecified
296.89	Bipolar II Disorder (Recurrent Major Depressive Episodes with Hypomanic Episodes)	F31.8	Other bipolar affective disorders
301.13	Cyclothymic Disorder	F34	Cyclothymia
296.80	Bipolar Disorder, Not Otherwise Specified	F31.9	Bipolar affective disorder, unspecified
293.83	Mood Disorder Due to a General Medical Condition	F06.xx	
292.84	Substance-Induced Mood Disorder		
		F34	Persistent mood [affective] disorders
		F38.0*	Other single mood [affective] disorders
		F38.8*	Other specified mood [affective] disorders
296.90	Mood Disorder, Not Otherwise Specified	F39	Unspecified mood [affective] disorder

* Note from World Health Organization (WHO) on this category: Any other mood disorders that do not justify classification to F30–F34, because they are not of sufficient severity or duration.

My Treatment Partnership Agreement

My Personal Treatment Goals

List your most important goals for treatment. Try to be as specific as possible. Try to avoid goals that are too general or vague. Ideally, the goals on your list should be reasonable and you should feel confident that you can achieve them with some effort.

_____

_____

_____

_____

Mood Monitoring

(Write down strategies that work for you to make sure you are able to do daily mood monitoring on a regular basis.)

_____

_____

_____

_____

Identifying Early Warning Signs of Depression or Mania

Important "red flags" that I should pay attention to:

For Depression:

_____

_____

For Mania:

_____

_____

Developing an Individual Coping Plan

(Specific steps I am going to take to make sure that my depression or mania doesn't get worse.)

For Depression

_____

_____

For Mania

_____

_____

Getting The Most Out of My Treatment: The Importance of Attending Therapy Regularly

I understand that in order for my treatment to be effective, I must plan on attending sessions regularly. It is likely that there will be times – good periods or bad periods – during which I will *not want* to attend regularly. Here are some of the things that may happen that will make it difficult to attend group regularly:

1. _____
2. _____
3. _____

Here is *my plan* to address the problems above and make sure that I do attend these treatment sessions regularly:

1. _____
2. _____
3. _____

The Importance of Taking My Medication

In addition to regularly attending psychotherapy sessions, it is very important that I continue seeing my psychiatrist and taking my medication regularly as prescribed. I understand that in order for medication to be effective, I must plan on taking my medication regularly. It's likely that there will be times – good periods or bad periods – during which I will *not want to* take my medication regularly. Here are some of the things that may happen (or have happened in the past) that will make it difficult to take my medication as prescribed.

1. _____
2. _____
3. _____

Here is *my plan* to address the problems above and make sure that I take my medication regularly as prescribed.

1. _____

2. _____

3. _____

Checking in With Important Others – Identifying and Using My Support System

I understand that there will be times that I will need to check in with significant others that I trust to make sure that I am doing OK. I have identified people below that have been helpful and supportive in the past and whom I agree to confide in before making important decisions about my life in periods where I may be experiencing an episode of mania or depression or significant mood shifts. If a question comes up in treatment about my decision-making or possible high-risk behaviors, I agree to consult with these people first before acting.

Name   Relationship   Telephone Number

_____

_____

_____

By signing this treatment partnership agreement when I am not seriously depressed or manic, it is my intention to prepare for periods of up and down moods in the future to help myself make better decisions and to remind myself of the value of using the tools and resources that I have identified above so that I can do a better job managing future depressed or manic episodes.

Signed _____ Dated _____

Sample Session Agenda Treating Bipolar Disorder

☐ Set session agenda

☐ Check-in using completed Mood Graph for past week (5–10 minutes)

☐ Review Home Practice assignments, including selected Automatic Thought Records.

Selected Interventions (Check all that apply):

☐ Working with family members to destigmatize the illness

☐ Working with family members to improve communication and problem solving

☐ Developing a crisis plan for times when patient is suicidal

☐ Coordinating with the doctor to develop a PRN medication for sleep problems/agitation

☐ Developing individual coping plans – mood monitoring skills

☐ Developing individual coping plans – identification of early warning signs

☐ Developing individual coping plans – developing and prioritizing specific coping strategies

☐ Coping with negative automatic thoughts – Automatic thought record

☐ Activity scheduling – pleasant events

☐ Graded task assignment

☐ Priority goal setting

☐ Developing structured activities and routines

☐ Strategies to reduce over-stimulation

☐ Other behavioral strategies _____

☐ Other cognitive strategies _____

☐ Using motivational interviewing to improve medication compliance

_____

☐ Assign home practice (homework) _____

Note: Sessions will have a flexible focus on core CBT skills for patients with bipolar disorder, depending upon their stage of treatment and level of acuity. Generally, the therapist should focus on at least one core skill set appropriate to the stage of therapy. In most sessions, the specific exercise chosen should be adapted to the needs of the individual as well as taking into consideration what would be most valuable in terms of skill review.

From: R.P. Reiser & L.W. Thompson: *Bipolar Disorder*   © 2005 Hogrefe & Huber Publishers

Mood Chart adapted from Basco and Rush (1996)

Name: Week of:		Mon	Tues	Wed	Thurs	Fri	Sat	Sun
Mood Graph								
Manic **+5** Extremely manic		•	•	•	•	•	•	•
+4 Very manic sig. problems functioning		•	•	•	•	•	•	•
+3 High		•	•	•	•	•	•	•
+2 High end of comfort zone		•	•	•	•	•	•	•
+1 Happier than usual		•	•	•	•	•	•	•
0 Middle of comfort zone	**Comfort zone**	•	•	•	•	•	•	•
-1 Lower than usual		•	•	•	•	•	•	•
-2 Low end of comfort zone		•	•	•	•	•	•	•
-3 Depressed		•	•	•	•	•	•	•
-4 Very depressed sig. problems functioning		•	•	•	•	•	•	•
-5 Extremely depressed		•	•	•	•	•	•	•
Hours of Sleep								
Other symptoms (0-10 rating)								

You may rate other symptoms such as irritability or agitation independently of mood using the rating scale above. Try to identify any important events that happened during the week that affected your mood.
Notes on events that caused mood shifts and any effective coping strategies used:

From: R.P. Reiser & L.W. Thompson: *Bipolar Disorder*
© 2005 Hogrefe & Huber Publishers

Identifying Signs of Depression or Mania

Domain	When I'm depressed	When I' manic
How I am feeling sad/blue anxious angry agitated ashamed happy elated irritable numb suicidal hopeless		
What I generally do level of social contact restlessness level of activity rapidity of speech withdrawal isolating sleep eating		
How I am thinking confidence level worry level negative thoughts ruminating obsessing worry about past worry about future concentration distractability feeling of competence general level of interest		
Physical problems energy level appetite level weight gain or loss interest in sex sleeping too much or too little		

From: R.P. Reiser & L.W. Thompson: *Bipolar Disorder*   © 2005 Hogrefe & Huber Publishers

Identifying Early, Middle and Late Signs of Depression or Mania

Domain	Early symptoms	Middle symptoms	Late symptoms
How I am feeling sad/blue anxious angry agitated ashamed happy elated irritable numb suicidal hopeless			
What I generally do level of social contact restlessness level of activity rapidity of speech withdrawal isolating sleep eating			
How I am thinking confidence level worry level negative thoughts ruminating obsessing worry about past worry about future concentration distractability feeling of competence general level of interest			
Physical problems energy level appetite level weight gain or loss interest in sex sleeping too much or too little			

From: R.P. Reiser & L.W. Thompson: *Bipolar Disorder*   © 2005 Hogrefe & Huber Publishers

Sample "Unhelpful Thought Record" – Weighing the Evidence

Situation (Give details of situation including who you were with, what happened, when it happened, etc.)

Thoughts	Feelings – Mood Rating	Alternative Thoughts – Countering Evidence	Change in Mood Rating
Helpful questions: What was going on in my mind at the time? What immediate images or memories did I have? What was I saying to myself at the time? What does this mean about how I view myself, my future, and the world around me? Are my thoughts "out of proportion" to the event?	1 word description of your mood with a 0-100 intensity rating, focusing on your strongest emotional response.	What is the evidence that this thought is true? What would other people say? What would I tell a friend in the same situation?	How did these alternative thoughts affect my mood?

From: R.P. Reiser & L.W. Thompson: *Bipolar Disorder*   © 2005 Hogrefe & Huber Publishers

Self-Help Resources

Books

Amador, X. (2000). *I am not sick, I don't need help! A practical guide for families and therapists.* Peconic, NY: Vida Press.

Burns, D.D. (1999). *Feeling good.* New York: Avon Books.

Burns, D.D. (1999). *The feeling good handbook.* New York: Plume Books

Copeland, M.E. (1994). *Living without depression and manic-depression.* Oakland, CA: New Harbinger.

Fuller Torrey, E. & Knable, M. (2002). *Surviving manic depression.* New York: Basic Books.

Granet, R., & Ferber, E. (1999). *Why am I up, why am I down.* New York: Dell.

Greenberger, D., & Padesky C. (1995). *Mind Over Mood.* New York: Guilford Press.

Jamison, K. (1995). *An unquiet mind.* New York: Alfred A. Knopf.

Miklowitz, D. (2002). *The bipolar disorder survival guide: What you and your family need to know.* New York: Guilford Press.

Scott, J. (2001). *Overcoming mood swings – a self-help guide using cognitive behavioral techniques.* New York: New York University Press.

Websites

http://www.dbsalliance.org/: Website for the Depressive and Bipolar Support Alliance (DBSA)

http://www.nami.org/: Website for National Alliance for the Mentally Ill

http://www.stepbd.org/: Website for the Systematic Treatment Enhancement Program for Bipolar Disorder

http://www.nimh.nih.gov/healthinformation/bipolarmenu.cfm: Website for National Institutes of Health

http://www.bipolarnews.org/: Website with information on life charting and bipolar disorder research

http://www.nlm.nih.gov/medlineplus/bipolardisorder.html National Library of Medicine – Medline research database on bipolar disorder

http://www.bpkids.org/: The Child and Adolescent Bipolar Foundation

http://www.bpso.org/: Bipolar Significant Others

Self-Help Organizations with Local Chapters

Depressive and Bipolar Support Alliance: A national support group that promotes education, research related to bipolar disorder, and sponsors local client run chapters and support groups

National Alliance for the Mentally Ill: A national support group that promotes education, research related to serious mental disorders, including bipolar disorder, and sponsors local chapters and support groups

Problem and Pathological Gambling

In the series: Advances in Psychotherapy – Evidence-Based Practice

James P. Whelan, Andrew W. Meyers

Over the past 30 years there has been a dramatic increase in the availability of convenient and legal gambling opportunities. Most people can reach a casino in a matter of a few hours, lottery tickets in minutes, or an online gaming site in seconds. Accompanying this proliferation of gambling is a growing understanding that between 5% and 9% of adults experience significant to severe problems due to their gambling activities. These problems have become a real health concern, with substantial costs to individuals, families, and communities.

The objective of this book is to provide the clinician – or graduate student – with essential information about problem and pathological gambling. After placing this behavioral addiction and its co-occurring difficulties in perspective, by describing its proliferation, the associated costs, and diagnostic criteria and definitions, the authors present detailed information on a strategy to assess and treat gambling problems in an outpatient setting.

They go on to provide clear and easy-to-follow intervention guidelines, including homework assignments, for a brief and cost-efficient cognitive behavioral approach to problem gambling, involving stepped care and guided self-change. Means of countering problems and barriers to change and vivid case vignettes round off this thorough, but compact guide for clinicians.

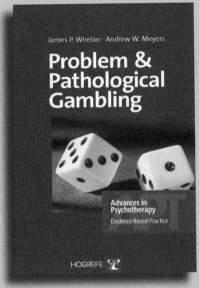

2005, ca. 104 pages, softcover
ISBN: 0-88937-312-4, US $ / € 24.95
Standing order price US $ / € 19.95
(minimum 4 successive vols.)
*Special rates for members of the Society of Clinical Psychology (APA D12) - Single volume: US $19.95
- Standing order: US $17.95 per volume
(please supply membership # when ordering)

Table of Contents

1. Description: Terminology and Definitions • Epidemiology • Course and Prognosis • Differential Diagnosis • Comorbidities • Diagnostic Procedures and Documentation
2. Theories and Models of the Disorder
3. Diagnosis and Treatment Indications
4. Treatment: Methods of Treatment • Mechanisms of Action • Efficacy and Prognosis • Variations and Combinations of Methods • Problems and Barriers to Change
5. Case Vignette
6. Further Reading
7. References
8. Appendix: Tools and Resources

Order online at: **www.hhpub.com**

HOGREFE

Heart Disease

In the series: Advances in Psychotherapy – Evidence-Based Practice

Judith A. Skala, Kenneth E. Freedland, Robert M. Carney

Despite the stunning progress in medical research that has been achieved over the past few decades, heart disease remains the leading cause of death and disability among adults in many industrialized countries. Behavioral and psychosocial factors play important roles in the development and progression of heart disease, as well as in how patients adapt to the challenges of living with this illness. This volume in the series *Advances in Psychotherapy* provides readers with a succinct introduction to behavioral and psychosocial treatment of the two most prevalent cardiac conditions, coronary heart disease and congestive heart failure. It summarizes the latest research on the intricate relationships between these conditions and psychosocial factors such as stress, depression, and anger, as well as behavioral factors such as physical inactivity and nonadherence to cardiac medication regimens. It draws upon lessons learned from a wide range of studies, including the landmark ENRICHD and SADHART clinical trials. It then goes on to provide practical, evidence-based recommendations and clinical tools for assessing and treating these problems. *Heart Disease* is an indispensable treatment manual for professionals who work with cardiac patients.

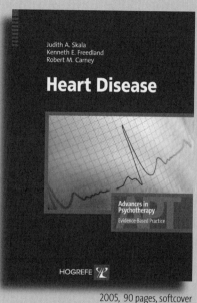

2005, 90 pages, softcover
ISBN: 0-88937-313-2, US $ / € 24.95
Standing order price US $ / € 19.95
(minimum 4 successive vols.)
*Special rates for members of the Society of Clinical Psychology (APA D12) - Single volume: US $19.95
- Standing order: US $17.95 per volume
(please supply membership # when ordering)

Table of Contents

1. Description: Terminology • Definition • Epidemiology • Course and Prognosis • Differential Diagnosis • Comorbidities • Diagnostic Procedures and Documentation
2. Theories and Models of the Disorder
3. Diagnosis and Treatment Indications
4. Treatment: Methods of Treatment • Mechanisms of Action • Efficacy and Prognosis • Variations and Combinations of Methods • Problems in Carrying out the Treatments
5. Case Vignettes
6. Further Reading
7. References
8. Appendix: Tools and Resources

Order online at: **www.hhpub.com**

HOGREFE

Childhood Maltreatment

In the series: Advances in Psychotherapy – Evidence-Based Practice

Christine Wekerle, Alec L. Miller, David A. Wolfe, Carrie B. Spindel

The serious consequences of child abuse or maltreatment are among the most challenging things therapists encounter. There has in recent years been a surge of interest, and of both basic and clinical research, concerning early traumatization. This volume in the series *Advances in Psychotherapy* integrates results from the latest research showing the importance of early traumatization, into a compact and practical guide for practitioners. Advances in biological knowledge have highlighted the potential chronicity of effects of childhood maltreatment, demonstrating particular life challenges in managing emotions, forming and maintaining healthy relationships, healthy coping, and holding a positive outlook of oneself. Despite the resiliency of many maltreated children, adolescent and young adult well-being is often compromised. This text first overviews our current knowledge of the effects of childhood maltreatment on psychiatric and psychological health, then provides diagnostic guidance, and subsequently goes on to profile promising and effective evidence-based interventions. Consistent with the discussions of treatment, prevention programming that is multi-targeted at issues for maltreated individuals is highlighted. This text helps the practitioner or student to know what to look for, what questions need to be asked, how to handle the sensitive ethical implications, and what are promising avenues for effective coping.

2005, ca. 104 pages, softcover
ISBN: 0-88937-314-0 , US $ / € 24.95
Standing order price US $ / € 19.95
(minimum 4 successive vols.)
*Special rates for members of the Society of Clinical Psychology (APA D12) - Single volume: US $19.95
- Standing order: US $17.95 per volume
(please supply membership # when ordering)

Table of Contents

1. **Description:** Terminology • Definitions • Epidemiology • Course and Prognosis • Differential Diagnosis • Comorbidities • Diagnostic Procedures and Documentation
2. **Theories and Models of the Disorder**
3. **Diagnosis and Treatment Indications**
4. **Treatment:** Methods of Treatment • Mechanisms of Action • Efficacy and Prognosis • Variations and Combinations of Methods • Problems and Barriers to Change
5. **Case Vignette**
6. **Further Reading**
7. **References**
8. **Appendix: Tools and Resources**

Order online at: **www.hhpub.com**

HOGREFE

Advances in Psychotherapy – Evidence-Based Practice

Developed and edited in consultation with the Society of Clinical Psychology (APA Division 12).

Pricing / Standing Order Terms

Regular Prices: Single-volume – $24.95; Series Standing Order – $19.95
APA D12 member prices: Single-volume – $19.95; Series Standing Order – $17.95
With a Series Standing Order you will automatically be sent each new volume upon its release. After a minimum of 4 successive volumes, the Series Standing Order can be cancelled at any time. If you wish to pay by credit card, we will hold the details on file but your card will only be charged when a new volume actually ships.

Order Form (please check a box)

[ ] I would like to place a Standing Order for the series at the special price of US $ / €19.95 per volume, starting with volume no. ....

[ ] I am a D12 Member and would like to place a Standing Order for the series at the special D12 Member Price of US $ / € 17.95 per volume, starting with volume no. ......
My APA D12 membership no. is:

[ ] I would like to order the following single volumes at the regular price of US $ / € 24.95 per volume.

[ ] I am a D12 Member and would like to order the following single volumes at the special D12 Member Price of US $ / € 24.95 per volume.
My APA D12 membership no. is:

Qty.	Author / Title / ISBN	Price	Total
		Subtotal	
	WA residents add 8.8% sales tax; Canadians 7% GST		
	Shipping & handling: USA — US $6.00 per volume (multiple copies: US $1.25 for each further copy) Canada — US $8.00 per volume (multiple copies: US $2.00 for each further copy) South America: — US $10.00 per volume (multiple copies: US $2.00 for each further copy) Europe: — € 6.00 per volume (multiple copies: € 1.25 for each further copy) Rest of the World: — € 8.00 per volume (multiple copies: € 1.50 for each further copy)		
		Total	

[ ] Check enclosed   [ ] Please bill me   [ ] Charge my: [ ] VISA   [ ] MC   [ ] AmEx
Card # _____ CVV2/CVC2/CID # _____ Exp date _____

Signature _____

Shipping address (please include phone & fax) _____

_____

_____

_____

_____

Order online at: **www.hhpub.com**

Hogrefe & Huber Publishers • 30 Amberwood Parkway · Ashland, OH 44805 • Tel: (800) 228-3749 · Fax: (419) 281-6883
Hogrefe & Huber Publishers, Rohnsweg 25 • D-37085 Göttingen, Germany, Tel: +49 551 49609-0, Fax: +49 551 49609-88
E-Mail: custserv@hogrefe.com

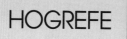